DAVID PIPER

THE
TREASURES
OF
OXFORD

DAVID PIPER

THE TREASURES OF OXFORD

PADDINGTON
PRESS LTD
NEW YORK & LONDON

Library of Congress Cataloging in Publication Data

Piper, David.
    Treasures of Oxford.

    Includes index.
    1. Oxford. University—Museums. 2. Oxford—
Museums. I. Title.
AM43.095P56   069'.09425'74   76-53314
ISBN 0-448-22836-X
First Printing March 1977
Second Printing May 1977

Copyright © 1977 David Piper
Printed in England by BAS Printers Limited, Wallop, Hampshire
Bound by Kitcat Ltd., London
Designed by Richard Johnson
Assisted by Patricia Pillay

IN THE UNITED STATES
PADDINGTON PRESS LTD.
Distributed by
GROSSET & DUNLAP

IN THE UNITED KINGDOM
PADDINGTON PRESS LTD.

IN CANADA
Distributed by
RANDOM HOUSE OF CANADA LTD.

IN AUSTRALIA
Distributed by
ANGUS & ROBERTSON PTY. LTD.

CONTENTS

INTRODUCTION

OXFORD IS ONE OF the oldest and most famous universities of the west. Since its foundation in the second half of the twelfth century, its visual character has gradually crystallised in an architecture of great beauty, picturesque and variety: of that aspect of Oxford, many accounts already exist. This book is concerned with treasures of the other visual arts—painting and sculpture, and the so-called applied arts—with which benefactors have endowed Oxford over the centuries. Donors may give for the sheer delight of adornment, or for the enhancement of scholarship—or, as happily so often is the case, in the interests of both; but perhaps most usually, gifts to Oxford are prompted by a simple, affectionate and grateful piety.

The first chapters here discuss the growth of these collections of treasures, from mediaeval times through the watershed of the Renaissance and the Reformation and on into our own days. From very early in their histories, the collections have accrued on two rather different kinds of institution. First, the University itself, the administrative body, containing the teaching faculties and—most important in this context—the great repositories of knowledge: the university library that came in due course to be called the Bodleian, and, from a little later, the various museums. The University also provides the theatre for the solemn and proper celebration of its own ritual—in degree ceremonies and so on—and in Oxford this literally is a theatre—Christopher Wren's Sheldonian in Broad Street.

The second kind of magnet for donors of objects of art is the colleges. These are not strictly part of the University, but virtually, in a great many respects, autonomous: a kind of federation of what began almost as lodging houses: hostels, with a presiding master and a handful of pupils. Towards the end of the

Middle Ages they began to grow, both in number and in material wealth that was manifest in the buildings, the furnishings of the chapels (especially stained glass and ritual plate), and the furnishing of more ceremonial communal meals (plate, salts, goblets, and so on).

But owing to the very close and personal relationship between pupil and tutor in each college, the attachments of piety and institutional loyalty were often stronger to the colleges than to the university, so that benefactions by grateful alumni have built up in all of them, while in each the enduring traditions are recorded and personified in sequences of memorial portraits of the Head of the House and its more celebrated dons (Fellows). Many of the college libraries have also built up collections that extend from books to drawings, prints and sculpture, of an importance far transcending the local needs of college teaching and research.

The first chapters deal also with the gradual sifting out of the University's collections, the story of the modulation and "shaking-out" of the holdings of the Bodleian Library and the Ashmolean Museum, up to the consolidation, in 1908, of the first Ashmolean departments under one roof and one administration. Following that, three chapters deal with the five departments that presently constitute the Ashmolean; to Antiquities and to Western Art, the first two, are now added the Cast Gallery, the Heberden Coin Room and Eastern Art. The other University collections are then grouped together, the Bodleian Library being here considered only very summarily as the repository of a great collection of illuminated manuscripts, and also of portraits. The other museums are not primarily concerned with art either, though art enters splendidly into all of them—the University Museum, the Pitt Rivers Museum, the Museum of the History of Science. These all have an even more specific teaching role than does the Ashmolean.

Two chapters are devoted to the colleges: one to Christ Church alone for reasons which are made apparent, and the second to the others—by no means to be dismissed carelessly as "the rest". Colleges, however, are still—as they were around A.D. 1300—hostels where teachers and students lead their private lives and conduct their own work, and for the colleges the art with which benefactors have endowed them is part and parcel of the texture of daily life. The colleges are not museums open to the public, though by courtesy specific parts of them—quads, gardens, chapels, and perhaps halls, even libraries—are frequently available on request. The indications here of the colleges' holdings are only summary, and very far from exhaustive.

The final chapter glances at the contributions newly added to the Oxford scene by two non-University institutions—the Oxfordshire County Museum, with its establishments at Woodstock and at St. Aldate's, and the Museum of Modern Art in

Pembroke Street—and also at that bonus to Oxford, Blenheim Palace, the grandest private house in England.

Oxford has a marvellous and inexhaustible richness of texture. Some of its treasures it displays for all to see, such as the magical long slow curve of the High from Magdalen Bridge up to Carfax, one of the great urban promenades in the world. Others it secretes, and the colleges are like oysters, their constituent traditions breeding pearls. It is all a continuing process, and when Oxford ceases to grow and to change, she will be dead—but meanwhile her powers of endurance and self-renewal seem sturdily vigorous. Thus, while this book was being completed, a curious ceremony took place involving the colossal heads of the Emperors that gird the Broad front of the Sheldonian Theatre. These heads went up originally when Christopher Wren built the Sheldonian, from around 1663. They were never portraits of specific Roman emperors, but rather tutelary presences. Gradually they entered into myth. By the 1850s, Verdant Green, the freshman hero of Cuthbert Bede's best-selling novel, was being

The Old Ashmolean (now the Museum of the History of Science). Probably designed by Thomas Wood, 1678–83. The Emperors' Heads were originally by William Bird; replaced by a new set in 1868 and again in 1972–76.

9

informed they represented the original heads of the colleges. Early in this century, as readers of Max Beerbohm's *Zuleika Dobson* will recall, they burst into a heavy sweat at first sight of that doomfully beautiful heroine—but by then they were no longer the originals, which, corroded by weather of two centuries, had been replaced by new ones in about 1868. These replacements, being carved in very soft stone, lasted a mere century. In the late 1960s they were adjudged expended and expendable, anonymous blurred masks stained with tears of liquid soot (though many preferred them so). The last four of the replacements (carved by Michael Black) were set up on a clear February day in 1976 under a chill metallic sky, with the aid of Morris dancers, free beer, a pinkish-grey life-size elephant ridden by two small boys, a twenty-foot high grotesque of a furious Proctor, and an unparticipating mutter of picketing strikers outside Blackwell's bookshop on the other side of the road. But they should hold for a century or so, and they are already incorporated into the Oxford treasury: I have already heard them identified by one tourist as Knights of the Round Table.

CHAPTER ONE

THE EARLY COLLECTIONS IN OXFORD

T HE CONCEPT OF ART collections, and especially their consolidation into museums, is a development of the Renaissance. In the Middle Ages, collections were built up in the monasteries, the cathedrals, the great churches and, to a more uncertain extent, in the royal palaces. On the whole the Church had a much firmer physical basis than the princes, who were peripatetic and more open to catastrophe by rebellion and war. Ecclesiastical collections centred on the embellishment of the fabric of God's houses—sculpture, stained glass, wall paintings (not really collections, but part and parcel of the architecture). They contained the furniture of the liturgy: the silver and gold of ceremonial vessels; the rich vestments of the priests for which England, through *opus anglicanum*, became famous; and, of course, books.

Books, though they are really outside the scope of this survey, have been accumulated by scholars of the University since the very beginning. The beautiful mediaeval books—illuminated bibles, breviaries, psalters, perhaps even a few courtly romances—must have been there. The surviving fabric of Merton College library dates from 1375–78, while at Balliol a significant part of the mediaeval collection remains. But generally the college manuscripts in Oxford colleges do not compare with the wealth of, say, Corpus Christi library at Cambridge. As far as the University is concerned, the great room built to house the books given by Humphrey, Duke of Gloucester, and finished in 1490, survives as the best-known part of the Bodleian Library. The original books vanished (only three are there now) in the disarray into which the University Library fell in the sixteenth century, until 1598 when Bodley, wearied of public and diplomatic life, "concluded at the last, to set up my Staff at the Librarie dore in Oxon . . . ."

By then the manuscript book had given way to the printed book. In fact, through a succession of rich gifts and bequests by later benefactors, the Bodleian has become one of the world's great treasure houses of illuminated manuscripts, not only Western but Oriental, and we shall take a glimpse, if but a very summary one, of that later on.

Outside the University, there were doubtless riches to be found in the larger monastic foundations: the Abbeys of Osney, of Abingdon and of Godstow, besides the smaller monastic colleges. But what there was almost all vanished in the Reformation and the Dissolution of the monasteries. Amongst them St. Frideswide survived fairly substantially to be embraced by Christ Church as captive cathedral, while Godstow, home of Benedictine nuns, is a shell of roofless walls by the Thames.

Besides illuminated books, some of the wealth that monastic houses (and therefore colleges) had, and which one might reasonably expect to survive, was their liturgical and domestic plate. Indeed, Gerald Taylor, author of a standard work on silver, has written that "Oxford has long been second only to London in the richness and variety of British plate in regular use within its boundaries". This wealth, however, is mainly of post-Restoration date; although the earlier pieces are far from negligible, most of them have come later by gift. The earliest college holdings were lost first in the sixteenth-century reforms, and then, probably more drastically, when the Royalists turned Oxford into their headquarters for all England in the Civil War between 1642 and 1646. The Royal Mint was set up in Oxford, and though this produced some historically fascinating coinage, the precious metals that went into that coinage tended to come from the melted-down plate of the colleges. The colleges' gifts to the royal cause were not all made with generous abandon, and the King's request was in fact an order—as both Exeter and St. John's discovered when they tried to take avoiding action. Yet Corpus Christi College did by some means manage to retain its stock, which still includes three pieces that belonged to the founder, Bishop Fox: his crozier of about 1490, a marvellously intricate piece of goldsmiths' work; a standing salt of about the same date; and his gold chalice and paten of 1507. These are pieces of very high quality and magnificent sophistication. New College too possesses a wealth of mediaeval silver which the college often keeps on public display. In the Chapel can be found William of Wykeham's crozier which is more than a century earlier than Bishop Fox's, and of a more austere though still highly elaborate distinction. Indeed, it is claimed to be the most splendid example of English goldsmith's work of this period in the country. It somewhat resembles a small portable shrine, with gabled niches peopled with exquisite little figures of saints and prophets—a vivid reminder of the wealth of figurative carving that the iconoclastic severity of the Reformation and then of the seventeenth-century Puritans swept for ever from the real shrines: the chantries, churches and cathedrals of mediaeval England.

Various colleges still own individual pieces of mediaeval plate associated—often rightly, sometimes wrongly—with the names of their founders. One of these is the founder's cup at Queen's College, said to have been given by Robert of Eglesfield (d. 1349): a buffalo horn with silver-gilt mounts inscribed *Wacceyl* (or Wassail, and indeed used as a loving cup), and a punning eagle poised melancholy-haughty on its lid, a convincing enough echo of the founder's name. Much college plate is seen only at college feasts or gaudies, where fellows and their guests use the plate by candlelight. Much of it serves as table decoration— the portly tankards, the fantastic salts, shining down the tables— but some is still functional: the candlesticks, the loving cup. The latter serves an archaic rite of friendship now forgotten in most places other than Oxford and Cambridge: the cup, filled, passing from hand to hand down the long tables, a little group standing indicating its whereabouts, bobbing little bows, drinking, wiping the rim of the cup after drinking, and one always standing protective at the drinker's back, so that no knife, unsolicited and hostile, shall enter it. Then the great dishes, gilt or silver-gilt basins, glinting their way down the tables likewise, laden with rose water in which the diners dip a corner of damask napkin and with it cool wine-fevered temples.

A kind of object (other than plate) associated directly with the founders of colleges, that one would expect to find in colleges, is the memorial portrait. The stratum of society to which early scholars looked for benefaction was very much that of the courtier—or administrative prelate. In the later Middle Ages, the way to preferment and power for those who were not born into the purple was through the Church. A boy from even quite humble background could make his way to the top—most spectacularly perhaps in the case of Wolsey. The drawback was that once there, he was denied the opportunity of founding a dynasty. The Church was celibate. The substitute for a personal dynasty could be an educational foundation, carrying the founder's name down through the centuries. To begin with, such a foundation would be an actual chantry, and an integral part of its beneficiaries' duties would be to pray daily, to chant in word and song for the soul of their founder. Even now, in college chapels and even at some college dinners, prayers for the founder and thanks for his benefaction are offered up regularly. The sustaining of such traditions becomes more vivid and more meaningful when the name of the founder can be associated with an image of his individual presence, with a portrait.

Most poignantly, this would be in the form of a tomb-monument with effigy. In the richly furnished chapel of Magdalen College, its founder, the great Bishop Waynflete himself, does appear, but in a subsidiary role as a supporting 'weeper' in the monument of his father, Richard Patten. This is of about 1450, but has only been in the chapel since 1823 when it was brought from Wainfleet. But I think the best example of a tomb monument is a relatively late one: the discreet monument, with twin effigies, to Sir Thomas and Lady Pope of about 1567 in Trinity College chapel.

Portraits sometimes took the form of a founder's statue set in the gateways of colleges. The finest of these are perhaps the fifteenth-century statues of the co-founders of All Souls, Henry VI and Archbishop Chichele (now removed to the undercrypt of the chapel), but it was a continuing if sporadic practice. Thus we see Wolsey at Christ Church, and, from the early seventeenth century, the co-founders of Wadham, Nicholas and Dorothy Wadham. (The present statues are copies of the originals.)

Paintings of founders are numerous, but in the case of the oldest colleges unlikely to be contemporary with their subjects. There is very little before 1500. For whilst in Northern Europe the art of naturalistic portraiture flowered first, with sudden and never-surpassed perfection, in the work of the Van Eycks, in Britain it came later and was generally in a relatively weak provincial derivation of the Van Eyckian idioms. The finest contemporary painting of a founder in Oxford (and indeed a masterpiece in the early history of painting in England) is the portrait of Bishop Fox at Corpus Christi, painted about 1520 by John Corvus (alias Raven), a Fleming immigrant from Bruges. The stylised and powerful rigour of his portrait of Fox—that carved and clenched composure of the austere shaven face brooding over the clasp of his hands on his staff—seems rather to look forward to the advent in England of the Swiss-German Holbein, almost a decade later, than back to the Van Eycks.

At Christ Church one might not expect to find such contemporary reflection of the person of the most sumptuous of all Oxford founders, Cardinal Wolsey, as he fell from grace before his Cardinal College was completed, but the virtually complete obliteration of Wolsey's collections everywhere by his triumphant monarch is both startling and sad. There are only two surviving types of portrait of Wolsey drawn from life, one known only by a later pencil copy in the Library at Arras, and the other a coarse, brutally bovine profile. Battered versions of this one (one or two of which may be contemporary) are in Christ Church, singularly unworthy memorials of one of the greatest prince-prelates of Renaissance Europe. Christ Church proceeded to celebrate him later, but the memorial recreations are shackled rather than inspired by the example proposed by that earlier image. One is the three-quarter-length painting (in Christ Church Hall) by Sampson Strong in about 1610, and another is a statue by Francis Bird dated 1719 (set up in its present niche on Tom Tower in 1872).

Sampson Strong was a widely employed instrument in the first wave of celebration of founders by retrospective memorial paintings. This coincided with the growth in England of a strong antiquarian interest. Sets of portraits of English monarchs were not uncommon in the sixteenth century, as were portraits of holders of an office, or a nobleman's ancestors. They illustrated the authenticity, the continuity, the legitimacy even, of an enduring tradition. In Oxford, Strong was briskly employed for about twenty years painting founders: these include William of Wykeham for New College (1596), Chichele for All Souls (1609), a copy of Fox at Corpus (1604), and Wolsey twice—once for Christ Church and once for Magdalen (where the inhabitants sometimes refer to the portrait's sitter as "a former bursar of this college"). Sampson Strong was not a distinguished painter, and his versions are more eloquent of institutional piety than of artistic merit or authentic likeness. His Wolsey still presides over Christ Church hall after nearly four hundred years.

On the other hand, as tastes and expectations changed through the centuries, the founder's image might be refurbished. Thus at All Souls, if you probe around, you can find the co-founder Chichele first, in the weather-worn statue already mentioned, all but contemporaneous; then Sampson's image, stiffly blessing; then—a century on—Sir James Thornhill's whole-length variation on the theme in a baroque key, perhaps about 1720; then (commissioned by the College in 1751, no doubt an ornament for the Codrington Library, completed that year), a marble bust by Roubiliac. But that is not the end of it: in the chapel, in a small window south of the great west window, flanked by excellent company, St. Augustine and St. Gregory—is a mediaeval stained-glass figure of Chichele.

Apart from the colleges, the University and its departments, especially the Bodleian Library, gradually accumulated sets of portraits—visual counterparts to the anthem *Let us now praise famous men*. This continues the practice, established in Renaissance Italy, of celebrating *uomini famosi*. The first sequence in Oxford was an enormous painted frieze of heads of poets, learned men and seers, starting with Aristotle and finding its climax in the singularly dour representations of Elizabethan Puritan divines. It was painted in the early seventeenth century around a ceiling in the upper floor of the Bodleian, then vanished in a reorganisation of 1830 and was only recently recovered and restored. Never much more than crude, the heads now have a battered but determined air.

To the Bodleian also came in the late seventeenth century a retrospective set of Founders of colleges painted by a competent professional called W. Sonmans. His likeness of John of Balliol (d. 1269) is said to be a portrait of a local blacksmith, while Balliol's wife Devorguilla was based on Jenny Reeks, daughter of an apothecary in the parish of St. Peter's, and "the famousest beauty in Oxford of her days". This set was engraved in mezzotint in the early eighteenth century, and sets of the engravings served as handsome gifts for distinguished visitors or prospective bene-factors to the University.

It was not only founders' portraits that were meant to remain for ever presiding over their particular places. More specialised, designed perhaps to stimulate the study of medicine, was a series of portraits, copied from originals elsewhere, of famous seventeenth-century physicians—Harvey, Sir Thomas Browne and others—given to the University by Humphrey Bartholomew of University College in 1735. A series of portraits of musicians, historically much more important, grew up in the Music School, which was once located in the southeast corner of the Old Schools Quadrangle. The group includes perhaps the finest and best-preserved example of English Elizabethan painting in Oxford: the portrait of the musician Dr. John Bull, aged 27 in 1589, at once vivid and melancholy with his skull and hourglass—characteristic of the reconciliation of a sitter's personal vanity and the vanity of that vanity, so typical of portraiture of the period. The portrait of the great Elizabethan historian Camden was originally intended to hang in the Old History School "over the Pew wherein the Professor reads": the medical set already mentioned hung in the Anatomy School, the musical ones in the Music School.

The persistent habit of recording each successive incumbent of an office or a post by his (and now her) portrait goes back a very long way. Many colleges still ritually observe the custom for the head of the house as he or she approaches retirement. In the Bodleian, the portrait of Thomas James, first Library-Keeper, was painted on his resignation in 1620; as this book is being written, Dr Robert Shackleton, the nineteenth in succession (through nearly four hundred years) of Bodley's Librarians, composes himself to the cool, uncompromising vision of Sir William Coldstream. The portrait of Sir Henry Savile, close friend of Bodley, benefactor of the new Library and founder of the Chair of Astronomy, was given by his wife in 1622 (a serenely dignified example of formal Jacobean portraiture, by Gheeraedts) and the constellation of portraits of distinguished astronomers that later came to accompany it included Flamstead and Halley.

The Bodleian Library collection extended far beyond the subject of local heroes. The growth over the years, by donations or bequests—ranging in size from a single portrait to a whole collection—has been continuous: one can only mention a few specimen examples. In 1661 Galileo's prime apprentice and successor, Viviani, sent a portrait of him to the University; in 1674 Dr Walter Charleton gave a marvellous thrusting whole-length of Sir Martin Frobisher, explorer of the Americas, pistol at the ready, painted by Cornelius Ketel in 1577; the painter Thomas Gibson gave his painting of a distinguished alumnus, the philosopher John Locke, in 1733; in 1701 Samuel Pepys commissioned Sir Godfrey Kneller to paint for the University the great mathematician John Wallis. Before 1737 a local collector, Dr. Rawlinson, gave near fifty portraits that he had collected.

The collection of portraits was therefore fairly comprehensive, and was attractive to potential donors because it was from the seventeenth-century largely housed in "The Public Gallery in the Schools in Oxon" which has claims to be called the first public gallery in Britain. Amongst the various branches of the art of painting and sculpture represented in Oxford, that of portraiture, through university, colleges, and university departments (with the exception of the Ashmolean Museum) is by far the most copiously represented.

The historical and iconographical importance of this wealth was saluted by the remarkable three-volume *Catalogue of Oxford Portraits*, compiled by Mrs. Reginald Lane Poole and published between 1912 and 1925. These volumes still constitute the essential index to portraits in Oxford, even though many additions have been made in the fifty years since and details of identification and attribution need revision. They were, and remain, a fine pioneering achievement. The first step in locating any portrait is therefore to Mrs. Poole, but after that it gets more difficult, especially where university, as distinct from college portraits, are concerned, as there has been considerable movement. Some of the most interesting portraits in the Bodleian have moved to the Ashmolean, and very few remain in areas of the Library open to the casual visitor, so that application must generally be made to the Librarian for an appointment to view.

Since about 1910, the "official" portrait gallery of the University has been the Examination Schools in the High Street. The splendour of the 1882 interior offered a suitable setting for the grander people—public faces in public places, royalty, aristocracy, Chancellors, robed and wigged, of the university, major benefactors. It also houses a grand if conventional range of whole-lengths of monarchs from William and Mary to Edward VII (when Prince of Wales) as an undergraduate at Christ Church. But there are also some odd exotics—a King of Prussia, a Tsar of Russia and, perhaps most intriguing for the connoisseur in this Victorian revival, a life-size whole-length of Lord Carlingford painted by J. J. Tissot in 1871, with an exquisite still-life of a mantelpiece with bronze clock, Japanese fans, bric-a-brac and a fine white bull-terrier. More typical, and excellent of its sober kind, is Jonathan Richardson's whole-length of 1730 of that archetypal British benefactor, Sir Hans Sloane, commodiously gowned and wigged, President of the Royal College of Physicians, President of the Royal Society, fabulous collector from whose hoards in 1753 emerged the British Museum itself. The portrait was given to Oxford by the sitter himself.

Most of the portraits hung through the colleges and the university are of the quality represented by that of Hans Sloane.

Jonathan Richardson: *Sir Hans Sloane*. Oil on canvas, 1730.

For contemporaries of the subject of any portrait, the first consideration was inevitably that it should be a good likeness (or, since agreement on that is rare, that it should generally be acceptable and recognisable); then, that it should betray neither its subject nor the needs of memorial piety, but should be decorous, and its quality as a work of art would contribute to that. For the student of subsidiary figures in the main stream of the history of British portraiture, Oxford is a very rich source, from the seventeenth century till now.

For the seventeenth and early eighteenth century, though Van Dyck is not represented, Lely and Kneller, his successors as the leading portrait painters, are. Whilst most successful portrait painters inevitably gravitate to the richest source of patronage, the moneyed and fashionable society of London, there are a number of painters especially associated with Oxford. Two of these are Isaac Fuller and John Taylor, who lived and worked in Oxford for a time. Sadly, however, the most gifted of English-born painters of the seventeenth century, William Dobson, is not represented though he spent the last four years of his brief life (1642–46) in Oxford, painting the embattled royalists.

Outside the Ashmolean Museum, the great figures of the so-called golden age of British portraiture—Reynolds, Gainsborough and Lawrence—are represented mainly (as we shall see later) in the precincts of Christ Church. Lawrence has some fine portraits in other colleges as well. But in general, it is to artists of the middle rank that university sitters seem to have gone: less expensive, of course, but also perhaps less hazardous for clients wishing to perpetuate their own identities rather than be transferred into creations of painters of genius—to remain Professor Jones or Dr. Smith rather than become the local Reynolds or Gainsborough. So there is much competent (and often, for the student, helpfully documented) work by painters like John Riley, Thomas Murray, Jonathan Richardson. There are the followers of Reynolds and Lawrence like Hoppner and Owen, and many Royal Academicians of the nineteenth century.

In spite of the existence of the photograph for nearly a hundred and fifty years, the colleges remain, both in Oxford and Cambridge, amongst the staunchest upholders of the tradition of portrait painting, and on the whole this patronage has shown courage. Primarily, it is the sitter that matters—from founders to famous old boys. The Oxford collections are the university equivalent of the National Portrait Gallery, where the over-riding consideration is the authenticity of the identification of the sitter and artistic quality, if any, a bonus of chance. No college has yet asked its Head to sit to Francis Bacon, the one British painter who offers an entirely revolutionary concept of what a portrait can be, but Coldstream, Patrick George and comparably austere talents were employed even before they became generally acceptable while some of the more traditionally-minded painters, John

Ward, Derek Hill, and others, have produced admirable work.

The colleges have rarely gone beyond the usual range of founders, college heads and old boys but the famous portrait in Christ Church, of a kitchen scullion or cook, painted by John Riley in about 1680, and that of Thomas Hodges, a grotesquely crippled "servant to the Chaplains Room", signed and dated by a mysterious "L.L." 1764, in New College, are exceptions. Oriel College has recently been presented, by Sir Weldon Dalrymple-Champneys, with a collection of portraits of the Champneys family and relations, and a new room to hang them in. The connection of the sitters with the college is generally tenuous, but the set is unusually decorative. But the most remarkable of all such sets of family portraits in the university is a much earlier one, that of the Tradescant family, which came with Elias Ashmole's original gift to Oxford in 1683. And it is to the growth of the institution that Ashmole launched on its devious way that we must now turn.

CHAPTER TWO

THE UNIVERSITY COLLECTIONS UP TO 1900

THE RECOVERY OF THE university library, after its refoundation as the Bodleian Library in 1602, was astonishing. Books and manuscripts poured in from benefactors, notably from that Earl of Pembroke whose bronze statue now stands outside the library, and from Archbishop Laud.

Objects other than books which were of interest to English academics after the Renaissance were also given to the university. Perhaps among the first of these were coins and medals. The earliest Oxford coin collection—formed by Edward Beaumont and left to Christ Church in his will of 1552—has now vanished, but John Barcham of Corpus gave his very rich collection of Greek and Roman coins, through Laud, to the university in 1636. The collection was housed in the Bodleian, which, along with the Ashmolean, was to remain for centuries a major repository for coins given to the university. It was augmented by sporadic gifts, amongst which a notable early one was that (prompted originally by Laud, though by then he was dead) from Sir Thomas Roe, of Greek coins, in 1644.

The same Sir Thomas Roe was an agent (if not a particularly willing one) in the formation of the Earl of Arundel's collection of Roman marbles which was indeed part of the first major art collection, in the modern usage of the term, to be formed by a private individual in Britain. Thomas Howard, Earl of Arundel (1585–1646) started his collections in 1606, when he restored his family's shattered fortunes by marriage to a rich wife. The part of it which was surely the most remarkable for sheer quality, the pictures and drawings, is dispersed for ever, mostly sold abroad after his death in exile. A significant residue of his classical marbles was not so conclusively scattered, and, in time, was to come together in Oxford, where it still forms the nucleus of the Ashmolean Museum's antiquities.

Although Arundel was one of the first in England to assess and collect works of art for their quality—"the father of Virtu in England"—he was also not one to be confined by aesthetic considerations. In his travels in Italy (where an early companion was Inigo Jones), he became an addict of antiquity. In Rome he began his collection of sculpture, even acquiring permission to excavate. It may be that some of the "finds" he made then had been specially planted for him by the obliging and cynical authorities—and the quality of the collection that survives is very mixed indeed—but in the end his collection of antique sculpture was remarkable for more than quantity: to take just one example, the fragment of "Homerus", a Hellenistic torso of the second century B.C. (now on loan to the Ashmolean from Fawley Court), is of admirable character, both sensitive and monumental.

The difficulties of exporting statuary out of Rome were fairly prohibitive, however, and Arundel began to look further afield, to the almost unexplored field of Greece and Asia Minor. These he never visited, but worked through agents, his agents being in turn aided by Sir Thomas Roe, appointed ambassador in Constantinople to the Sublime Porte in 1621. Not all projects succeeded: Roe's attempts to buy half the reliefs from the propylon of the Porta Aurea of Constantinople failed, as did a determined Arundelian snatch at the great Egyptian granite obelisk from the Circus of Maxentius (that stayed in Rome, a little later to crown Bernini's Fontana dei Fiumi in the Piazza Navona). But the statuary flooded into London, especially from Arundel's young chaplain William Petty, working, with Roe's support, about the literal of Asia Minor—Pergamon, Samos, Ephesus, Chios. He suffered shipwreck and imprisonment as a spy, yet he managed to snap up a remarkable collection of inscriptions at Smyrna, formed by an agent of the French scholar de Peiresc when the agent was imprisoned. By the late 1650s the sculpture collection at Arundel House held around thirty-seven statues, one hundred and twenty-eight busts, two hundred-odd inscriptions, plus various sarcophagi and fragments. As early as 1626, Francis Bacon was seen in the garden there, "where were a great number of Ancient Statues of naked Men and Women", making "a stand, and as astonish'd cryed out: *The Resurrection!*".

Arundel's antiquities, unlike his paintings and drawings, were of course too cumbersome to transport to Antwerp when he left England for ever in 1642. Their history after his death in 1646 became muddled and unwholesome. Remaining mainly at Arundel House, they seem to have survived its occupation by a Roundhead garrison, but after that, Arundel's grandson was uninterested. Decay and positive abuse followed—part of the famous Marmor Parium (of which the major fragment is now in the Ashmolean) served as a hearth-stone. About half of the inscriptions—over a hundred of them—were already lost when the diarist John Evelyn, in 1667, intervened with their owner. "These previous monuments when I saw miserably neglected & scattered up & downe about the Gardens and other places of Arundell House, & how exceedingly the corrosive aire of London Impaired them, I procured him to bestow on the University of Oxford . . . ." The University accepted gratefully and everything, except statuary, was removed to Oxford. The bulk of the gift consisted of inscriptions. These had in part been published, very swiftly after their arrival in England, by the great scholar John Selden (*Marmora Arundeliana*, 1628), but a new publication was now promoted by the enriched university (Humphrey Prideaux, *Marmora Oxoniensa*, 1676). Unfortunately, amidst all this grateful care, it was not realised that while Oxford's air was not so swiftly corrosive as London's, in the long-term it would do significant damage. So the inscriptions were built into the walls that gird the Sheldonian precinct, and there weathered away until the mid-nineteenth century when they were finally brought indoors into the Ashmolean.

Before then, other elements had already come to the University. The Arundel sculpture stayed on at Arundel House in the Strand. Then part of it was sold to the Earls of Pembroke at Wilton House, when Arundel House was demolished, but the remainder seems to have been more or less stacked in a part of the grounds that became something of a quarry for builders. However, in 1691, Arundel's descendant the Duke of Norfolk sold most of the significant pieces left to Sir William Fermor, gave away a few to a family servant and had the residue dumped on waste ground by the Thames at Kennington. The pieces bought by Fermor were used as decoration in the garden or conservatory of his new house built by Hawksmoor at Easton Neston. There the malicious Horace Walpole in due course noted "a wonderful fine statue of Tully haranguing a numerous assembly of decayed emperors, vestal virgins with new noses, Colossus's, Venus's, headless carcases and carcasless heads, pieces of tombs and hieroglyphics . . . ." Some of them were in fact "restored" by Guelfi, Lord Burlington's favourite sculptor imported from Italy. In 1753, on the decay of the Fermor (Earls of Pomfret) fortunes, the Dowager Countess Pomfret bought the sculpture from her hard-pressed son and presented it, two years later, to the University of Oxford. The University gave thanks, commissioned a new account of its now augmented marbles (Richard Chandler, *Marmora Oxoniensa*, 1763), and put its new acquisitions into the Old Schools. There they stayed till their translation in the 1870s and 1880s into the new Ashmolean building. It was only a fraction of all Arundel's original statuary but nevertheless consisted of fifty-one statues, twenty-two busts or heads, and thirty-nine other pieces.

The fate of other surviving portions is discussed in detail in D. E. L. Haynes's full and entertaining account (*The Arundel Marbles*, Ashmolean Museum, 1975). Some pieces (including the "Homerus") that came to Fawley Court are now on loan to the Ashmolean; one of the later additions to the Ashmolean holding is a late Hellenistic head of a boy, unearthed by a workman in a Surrey Street basement (i.e. on the Arundel House site) in 1891, and intercepted by Judge Snagge who promptly bought it for a sovereign. Others are scattered—at Chiswick, in the British Museum, and so on—while the final scooping out of the Arundel House site on the Strand for a vast 1970s development revealed fresh finds.

The quality, as noted, is various. As the relentless pursuit of scholarship has divested so much once thought to be Greek of its originality, and proposed it as Roman copying, the fragments that now people the Randolph Gallery in the Ashmolean may not stir some visitors' imagination as once they did. And indeed the figure that Walpole noted as "a wonderful fine statue of Tully haranguing" still presides (though no longer identified as Cicero) over its colleagues in the Ashmolean; it is of continuing fine dignity. Familiarity will breed respect for the others, as they take their place in the reconstructed history of classical sculpture from the fifth century B.C. to the fourth century A.D. Their pedigree invests them with faint echoes of Aegean tides, and the memory of William Petty exploring for them some three hundred and fifty years ago, as he "encounters all accidents with so unwearied patience; eates with Greeks on their worst dayes; lyes with fishermen on plancks, at the best; is all things to all men, that he may obtayne his ends, which are your lordships service".

The story of the Arundel marbles goes far beyond the actual foundations of the Ashmolean Museum, though the Arundel inscriptions came in part to Oxford before the Museum. Ashmole did not endow the university with the nucleus of its museum collections until the late seventeenth century, but the chief constituent of his gift had started accumulating at much the same time as Arundel began, in the second decade of the century. Its originators were the Tradescants who came from Suffolk. Both John Tradescant the Elder (d. 1638) and John the Younger (1608–62) were celebrated gardeners, and the heart of their collection was trees and plants. They seem first to have introduced to Britain such enchantments as the lilac, the acacia, the occidental plane, and a great many others. The garden in the Tradescant house at Lambeth was no doubt a nursery and a market garden, and the first catalogue of it was printed in 1634; only a single proof copy of that survives. The second Tradescant catalogue, of 1656, was both printed and published, and, while most of it is taken up by the catalogue of plants, the introduction makes it clear that the emphasis has shifted. The essential matter is now

E. de Critz(?): *John Tradescant the Younger* in his garden, *c.*1650.

E. de Critz(?): *John Tradescant the Elder.* Probably painted some time after the sitter's death (1638).

23

"a *Catalogue* of *Rarities* and *Curiosities* which my *Father* has scedulously *collected*, and my *selfe* with continued diligence have *augmented* . . . ." The justification for publication is to convey *"an honour to our Nation, and a benefit to such ingenious persons as would become further enquirers into the various modes of Natures admirable workes, and the curious Imitations thereof . . . ."*

Today, such a purpose might be summarised as "an instrument for scientific research". The materials are divided into two sorts. First, the *Naturall*, birds, beasts, and fishes; shells, insects, "Outlandish-Fruits". The entries read like incantations:

Penguin, which never flies for want of wings
Puffin
Pellican
Shoveller
Tropic bird
Apous
Fulica
Dodar, from the Island *Mauritius*; it is not able to flie being so
   big
Birds of Paradise, or Manucodiata; whereof divers sorts,
   some with, some without leggs. . . .

With its emphasis on curiosities and on rarity, the Tradescants' collection was in the mediaeval tradition, tending to the miscellaneous, the exotic, the magical.

On the other hand, the classification of the second sort, *Artificialls*, by categories, looks forward to the method adopted, and still largely in use, for the ethnographical collections in the Pitt Rivers Museum in the late nineteenth century: "Vtensills, Householdstuffe, Habits, Instruments of VVarre used by several Nations, rare curiosities of Art &c. . . ."; under such labels you might find whole showcases displayed in the Pitt Rivers. Under *Mechanick artificiall Works in Carvings, Turnings, Sowings and Paintings*, Tradescant recorded:

Cornelian thum-cases of the Turks. Several curious paintings
in little forms, very antient. Splene-stones, divers sorts. The
Indian lip-stone which they were in the lip [*sic*]. . . . Two
figures carved in stone by Hans Holbein. . . . A Cherry-stone
with a dozen of wooden-spoons in it. A dozen of silver
Spoons in a little box. Flea chains of silves [*sic*] and gold with
300 links a piece and yet but an inch long. A small Landskip
drawn by Sir Nath: Bacon. The figure of a Man singing,
and a Woman playing on the Lute, in 4° paper; the shadow
of the worke being *David's* Psalmes in Dutch.

The category Variety of Rarities is particularly eccentric— "Indian fiddle. Spanish Timbrell. . . . Birds-nests from *China*. India Conjurors rattle, wherewith he calls up Spirits. Indian *PaGod* . . . Blood that rained in the Isle of Wight, attested by

Sir Jo: Oglander. A Hand of Het usually given to Children, in Turky, to preserve them from Witchcraft . . . ."

Much of all this was given to the Tradescants. The list of benefactors printed at the end of the catalogue has over a hundred names, starting with Charles I and his queen. But much too must have been collected by the Tradescants themselves, father and son, for both were travellers. John the Elder went to Flanders, France, the Barbary Coast and the Mediterranean, and Russia (the diary of his voyage to Russia in 1618 survives). He brought back plants with him, but surely also curiosities ("Duke of *Muscovy's* vest wrought with gold upon the breast and armes. Shooes from *Russia* shod with iron. Shooes to walk on Snow without sinking.") At one point, a pinnace from the ship went off to Greenland, and thence presumably came the "Match-coat from Greenland of the Intrails of Fishes. . . ." John the Elder did not go to America, although in 1625 he was asking for all manner of curiosities and plants from there to be sent to him, but his son went thrice, in 1637, 1642 and 1654. He even established perhaps rather shaky rights to land in Virginia. But plants were still his main interest (saluted by a memorial window to him, given recently by the Garden Club of Virginia to the Old Ashmolean building in Broad Street), and he undoubtedly brought many varieties new to England back with him. Other things came too, either direct or by gift from voyagers aware of the Tradescant interest. The most notable survivor, Powhatan's cloak, is listed in 1656 as "*Pohatan*, King of *Virginia's* habit all embroadered with shells, or Roanoke." It is to form the centre piece of a new display of Antiquities—a skin, all patterned indeed with shells, in which explorers once saw Pocahontas's father plain.

John the Younger was twice married, but his two children, a boy and a girl (both by his first marriage) had no offspring and the boy died in 1652. The future of the collections was therefore in doubt, and it is at this juncture that Elias Ashmole, antiquary, virtuoso, collector and diarist, appears on the scene. It seems from his diary that Ashmole first visited the Tradescant house in 1650, but fairly rapidly became closer acquainted and indeed helped with the Catalogue of 1656. The interpretation of subsequent events is controversial. What is certain is that in December 1659 a Deed of Gift, signed by John Tradescant and his wife Hester, made over to Elias Ashmole the Tradescant Closet of Rarities. It is equally certain that in April 1661, when Tradescant made his will, he bequeathed the Closet "to my dearly beloved wife Hester Tradescant during her naturall life, and after her decease I give and bequeath the same to the Universities of Oxford or Cambridge, to which of them she shall think fit." A year later he died, and thereafter much is murky and uncertain.

The widow Hester denied the validity of the Deed of Gift, but was contradicted by the Lord Chancellor (Clarendon) who resolved the suit that Ashmole brought against her in Ashmole's

favour. In October 1674 he had bought the house next door to Mrs. Tradescant and moved in as neighbour; next month he had started to transfer the collection to his house from hers—with her agreement, according to his diary. In September 1676, Hester Tradescant was signing a recantation, ordered upon her by the law, of various "calumnies" she had spread about concerning Ashmole's actions and behaviour. In 1677 he offered the University of Oxford the collection, together with his own collection (chiefly coins and his library), with the proviso that Oxford build a suitable home in which to house it. Oxford obliged, and one of the most handsome buildings in Oxford went up in Broad Street. Meanwhile, a disturbing entry occurs in that singularly chill and opaque document that is Ashmole's diary: 4 April 1678, 11.30 a.m.—"My wife told me, Mrs. Tradescant was found drowned in her pond. She was drowned the day before about noon, as appeared by some circumstances." However, Ashmole's building was finished in 1683, and he duly noted in his diary: "The last load of my Rarities sent to the barge. This afternoon I relapsed into the gout." On 20 March 1683, Wood, observing at Oxford, likewise noted: "Twelve cart-loads of Tradeskyn's rarities came from Mr. Ashmole at London to his new elaboratory at Oxon."

Thus the Tradescant collection, sometimes known as the Ark, was launched upon Oxford's history. Both Tradescants and Ashmole wished it so, but the fame and certainly the name remained mostly Ashmole's; he died in 1692, and was buried in Lambeth Church under an inscription that proclaims his name shall live as long as the Ashmolean Museum lives. Outside the church is the tomb of the three John Tradescants, grandfather, son, and grandson. The inscription on it claims for them, both less locally and more warmingly, an even more enduring immortality and one in perhaps an even nicer place . . . .

Whilst they (as Homer's Iliad in a nut)
A world of wonders in one closet shut,
These famous Antiquarians that had been
Both Gardiners to the Rose and Lily Queen,
Transplanted now themselves, sleep here: and when
Angels shall with their trumpets waken men,
And fire shall purge the world, these three shall rise
And change this Garden then for Paradise.

It is difficult, on the evidence available, to know whether one is being unfair to Ashmole. Although he is amongst the earliest English diarists—a contemporary of Pepys and Evelyn, and known to both of them—his diary conserves little that is agreeable about him. He married three times and each time the circumstances look somewhat suspicious, the material profit considerable. Evelyn thought him not learned, but industrious. His *History of the Order of the Garter* is thorough, copious and dry, and still a standard work: an anatomy of a particular pomp and

OPPOSITE: John Riley: *Elias Ashmole*. 1683. The frame is by Grinling Gibbons.

circumstance. It is difficult to warm to Ashmole and this wariness may be borne out by the visual evidence of the Founder's Room in the Ashmolean Museum. There hang Ashmole's portraits, both by John Riley, and those of Charles II and James II, all given or bequeathed by Ashmole. Amongst late Stuart portrait painters, Riley, whilst working according to conventional designs and poses, is justly praised for his sensitivity to the atmospherics of the individual face amongst the claustrophobic trappings of draperies and wig. The three-quarter-length of Ashmole, in its superb frame (probably by Grinling Gibbons himself) has official pomp—not just wig and formal draping but the gold chains and medals given by royalty (the originals of which, almost audible in their harness clink, are displayed in a glass case below). The face, amongst all the little paraphernalia, is convincing as an old man's face, eyes a little swimmy and faded. He looks both pompous and almost touchingly lonely. By way of contrast, the group of Tradescant portraits in the same room, reconciled in that one space, are both touching and startling. There is John the Elder, in a floral and vegetable painted oval; John the Younger, in a garden landscape, one large hand resting on his spade; and again, accompanied by a friend with a weird face with a squashed nose, and a huge pile of dazzling tropic shells alongside; then his wife, Hester, née Pooks, with her stepson and stepdaughter, she in tall steeple hat. In the general stream of Stuart society portraiture, these are extraordinary for the eccentricity of their dress, pose, and informality; they are also extraordinary in their quality and the enigma of their authorship. They are perhaps by Emmanuel de Critz, otherwise known by little other than documentary references, but that it should still be impossible to attribute pictures of such quality is very puzzling.

The manuscript *Statutes, Orders and Rules* that Ashmole drew up for the new institution outlined its purpose in full accordance with the view Tradescant set out in his introduction to the *Museum Tradescentianum*. Regulations as in the first printed notice, of 1714, provide for administration, cataloguing, security, hours and terms of admission—fees were charged according to the time spent in the Museum, though special rates applied according to the number of visitors in the group. This notice is still posted in the present Ashmolean Museum, but only as a curiosity. Ashmole expressed a wish that any profits should go to increasing the collections and their continuing growth was envisaged from the beginning. From the beginning too, usual museum problems occurred—security being one of the earliest. In 1688, John Aubrey gave various objects; only three years later a letter seems to indicate the loss of two of them, a Cooper miniature of Aubrey himself, and a Hilliard of Archbishop Bancroft. There were also gains, however—amongst them what is perhaps the most famous single object in the Museum, the ninth-century "Alfred Jewel", that magical image in gold, rock crystal and enamel, dug up near Athelney in Somerset, and bequeathed by Nathaniel Palmer in 1718.

The Museum, however, was not a very lively institution as such in the first century and a half of its existence, though it was very much active on other fronts. The collections consisted of: the Tradescant nucleus, much of it decaying inexorably; Ashmole's own contributions, notably of coins supplementing the numismatic (mainly medallic) part of the Tradescants' collection; and of books and manuscripts, to which were added the important gifts of Anthony Wood and John Aubrey. Natural history, antiquity, ethnography were represented, but Anthony Wood, describing the institution in 1683 as an "elaboratory", was right. The vital element in the Ashmolean to begin with resided in the chemical laboratory and its lecture room. Art as such was hardly associated with the Ashmolean until it moved house to Beaumont Street in the mid- and late nineteenth century. Well over half of the first printed catalogue, 1836, is concerned with natural history.

It was as the centre of the study of the sciences that the Ashmolean first flourished. By the mid-nineteenth century, that study began to expand so rapidly in sophistication and in variety that the old Museum building in Broad Street could no longer contain it. John Phillips, Keeper of the Ashmolean from 1855, was a geologist of great distinction; to his Keepership he added a Professorship and the Curatorship of the new University Museum, founded in 1855. To the University Museum, in its astonishing new building in the Parks, Phillips transferred the natural history collections; then, when the Pitt Rivers Museum opened in 1885, most of the ethnographic material went to that institution. These two moves must have involved most of what remained of the Tradescant collections: the items classifiable particularly as rarities and curiosities seem to have lost all respect as objects worthy of serious consideration, let alone of exhibition, by some time around 1820; in 1880, what seems to have been a considerable cache of them, not mentioned at all by the 1836 catalogue, was rediscovered "in a sort of outhouse easily accessible to passers-by in the street".

Meanwhile art, and also archaeology, were attracting attention elsewhere. The Arundel and other marbles seemed not to be worthily displayed, and gifts—from Dr. Randolph in 1796, from Sir Roger Newdigate between 1776 and 1805—provided capital for building the new so-called University Galleries. These were united in one project with the building of the new Taylorian Institute (for the study of modern languages) on a site on the corner of Beaumont Street and St. Giles. The brief was that "externally, the two buildings shall harmonise and, if possible, form parts of one architectural design, which is required to be of a Grecian character". The architect was C. R. Cockerell, and his building (1841-5) is indeed coherently harmonious, and its character distinctly Greek—an inspiration drawn considerably from the temple of Apollo Epikouries at Bassae. In the history of the Greek revival movement it is very late, but is certainly, in the crisp and bold modelling of its white and honey-coloured stone, one of the most brilliant examples of that movement. Into it came not only the gradual transfer of the marbles, but fresh gifts to the University: the immensely important Sir Thomas Lawrence/Woodburn collection of drawings by Michelangelo and Raphael (1846); the Chambers Hall antiquities, paintings and prints (1855); the Ruskin School bringing art students and live models, plus the drawings and watercolours given by Ruskin (1861–71); the Fox-Strangways gift of early Italian paintings (1850); the Douce collection (1863); the casts gradually accumulated for the Lincoln Professor of Classical Archaeology and Art from 1881.

Archaeology meanwhile was gathering strength rapidly in the Museum in Broad Street, as the romantic pursuit of antiquity for its own sake became tempered through the nineteenth century by the application of scientific method both to the objects themselves and to their excavation. The passionate surge of interest was far from restricted to academic and scholarly enquiry. It is difficult now to realise the amazement with which Victorian society confronted the revelations that controlled excavations made possible. The Museum had acquired the important Douglas collection from Sir Richard Colt Hoare as early as 1829, but the insistence on the importance of the collections to classical and historical academic study was part of the life-work of Greville John Chester between 1865 and 1892.

The world, so many still cosily but uncritically thought, had been created by God in seven days around 4000 B.C. The actual unimaginably huge time-span of the world, let alone of the universe, that the theories of Darwin and the archaeologists gradually established as inarguable, inspired vertigo and fear in some, but an urgent thirst for knowledge—for the exploration and charting of the past—in others.

Two of the greatest names in English archaeology, father and son, are closely associated with the Ashmolean. Sir John Evans' (1823–1908) great collection, including several thousand implements, stone and bronze, of the Palaeolithic, Neolithic and Bronze Ages, was given by his son, Sir Arthur Evans, in 1927. Sir Arthur Evans (1851–1941) was in fact the virtual second founder of the Ashmolean Museum. At first he was in alliance with a rich benefactor, C. D. E. Fortnum—one of those determined benefactors, refusing absolutely to be refused. Arthur Evans was appointed Keeper in 1884, and found the Ashmolean, still in Broad Street, in a most deprived condition: the natural history and ethnological collections had gone or were going; already in 1858 the coins had been removed to join those in the Bodleian and to the Bodleian too had gone Ashmole's books and manuscripts; the old Tradescant Gallery had been stripped of its panelling, the portraits of benefactors stacked in an attic in the

Clarendon Building; and the room itself was used for examinations (then a recently innovated pursuit). Evans remained Keeper for twenty-four years; by the time he resigned, at the end of 1908, the holdings of the old Ashmolean had all left the building in Broad Street for the former University Galleries, now considerably expanded on the north, in Beaumont Street. The archaeological collections of the University were consolidated there in one place, and so too was art—at least western art (eastern art and coins were added later). The two constituent departments, of antiquities and of western art, were united in the care of a single board of trustees, the Visitors of the Ashmolean Museum.

The Ashmolean Museum. South Front. By C. R. Cockerell, 1841–5.

CHAPTER THREE

THE ASHMOLEAN MUSEUM

DEPARTMENT OF ANTIQUITIES

THE ASHMOLEAN OF THE 1970s would startle any visiting ghost from the 1870s. In the nineteenth century, the exhibits had been seen in the light of a classical culture, predominantly literary, rooted in the study of Greek and Latin texts. The material objects tended to be seen as illustrations for these texts, and no doubt the most valued amongst them were those that themselves had come first—the inscriptions. The pattern of controlled excavations that started in the mid-nineteenth century—and which still, interrupted though it has been by armed conflict, persists throughout the world—has changed the emphasis of the collections fundamentally. Much of their contents now is not merely illustration to the history of the past, it is the very stuff of that history, and, after the British Museum, the Ashmolean is probably the richest museum in Britain for this material, in its variety, scope and intensity. Some of this richness is held in reserve in the study collections. This archive the aesthete is not compelled to see—though if he wish to do so, it is all controlled by numbering and by card-indexes, and will, on the sensitive register of the trained and experienced mind, read in part as the plotting points charting the slow curve of time itself.

Even so, a great deal in the displays of antiquities in the public galleries may seem, if one is not archaeologically inclined, both repetitious and of doubtful artistic quality. This is undoubtedly so, but I suspect it may well be healthy for a more purely aesthetic sensibility to be exposed to these hazards from time to time: it reminds one that, amongst other things, the distinction between "fine art", "applied art", "craft", even pots and pans, is a fairly artificial one. In some circles it has become, in the years since the war, almost improper to mention fine art. Of course,

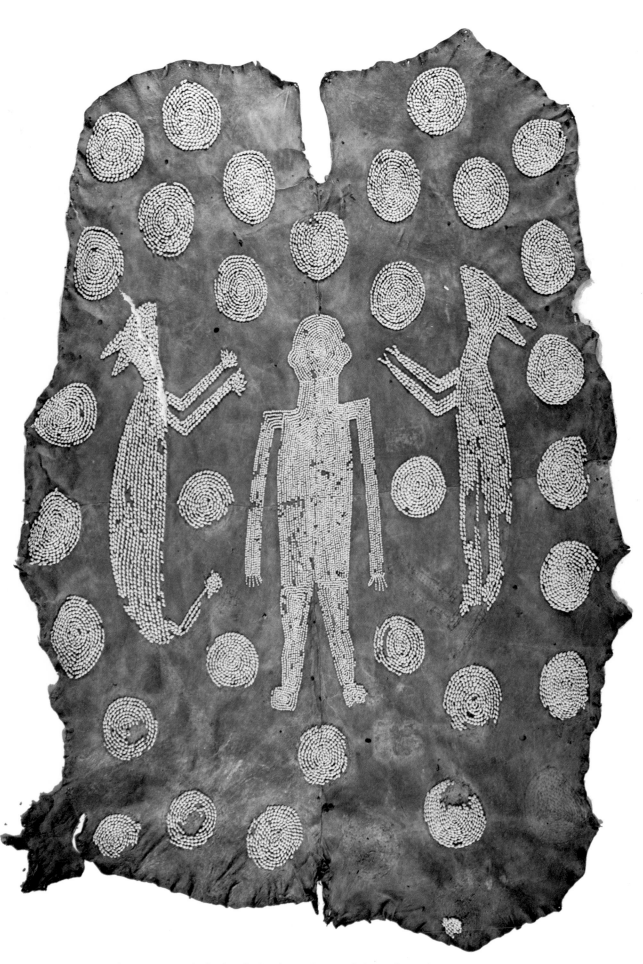

II. The ceremonial cloak of Chief Powhatan, father of Pocahontas.
Early seventéenth century.

III. PIERO DI COSIMO *A Forest Fire*. Panel, *c.* 1487–9.

Cy commence vng moult notable et deuot traitie
Intitule · Les douze fleurs de tribulation· prologue·

A Sa chiere anne en ihesucrist ses loiaulz
anne en nreseigne salut et confort En
celluy qui tous les desconfortez reconforte
Sicomme dit la sainte escripture Nulz ne
pouult loialment amer en lamour de charite cest
de ihesucrist se il na ioye de tous les biens qui a la
sainte ame poeuent aidier de venir a nreseigneur
Et se il nest doulent de cœur par compassion de
tous les maulx corporelz et espirituelz q la deftobet
de paruenir a la ioye du ciel Sicome saint pol le
tesmoingne quant il dit · Gaudere cu gaudentibz
et flere cum flentibus· Mais ilz sont aultres gens

VIII. GIORGIONE(?) *Virgin and Child*. Oil on panel, *c.* 1500–05(?).

IV. PAOLO UCCELLO *A hunt in the Forest.* Oil on panel, *c.* 1460/70(?).

V. Egyptian wall painting, fragment *Nefer-nefru-aten and Nefer-nefru-rē, daughters of Akhenaten*. Eighteenth dynasty, *c.* 1370 B.C.

VI. The Alfred Jewel, perhaps made for King Alfred (A.D. 849–99).

VII. China. Two celadon bowls: Sung (A.D. 1300–1500), and Yüan (A.D. 1500–1600).

this does not mean that the delicate aesthete has ceased to exist, only that the range of objects to which delicate aestheticism directs its attention has vastly enlarged.

The extension of the range is pure gain. Take, for instance, the *shawabtis*, those odd mini-mummies—sometimes subtle, but often clumsy, often indeed individually repulsive—that peopled so many Egyptian tombs from the Middle Kingdom onwards. They are only a few inches tall, made sometimes of stone but more often of clay (some mass-produced from moulds) or faience, and often of a vivid blue. These figures are the stand-ins, the substitutes for their originals of flesh and blood. For the historian, the *shawabtis* yield names and duties of individuals, information about rank and social, ceremonial, or agricultural habits, etc. But to the privateering imagination of the raiding artist they may yield quite other things. There is a fine case of them in the Ashmolean, a whole squad or platoon for ever at attention, still alert after three or four thousand years. A modern artist interested in patterns of repetition might simply sign the whole case and claim it as his own.

The display of antiquities in the Ashmolean is not strictly chronological, for the collections have grown up often in conflict with the logic of the architecture of existing buildings and the limitations of a constricted and finite site—and alas, usually those of limited finance. Thus, on entry to the Ashmolean you have, on the ground floor, the Greek and Roman statuary in a long handsome gallery that suits the theme admirably: beyond that are not only the Egyptian collection but Viking remains and the British Middle Ages, including objects up to as late as the sixteenth century. If you want to see the Alfred Jewel, perhaps the best-known object in the whole Museum, and nothing else, that's where it is.

On the first floor, at the top of that steep but grand main staircase there hang the mute and enigmatic portraits of Ashmole and the Tradescants. These I have already described briefly (page 28). Accompanying them are two cabinets displaying small curiosities that can be identified with entries in the 1656 catalogue—from Nathaniel Bacon's little landscape (said to be the earliest painted in England by an Englishman) to carved Chinese balls-within-balls, from a miniature painting of the elder Tradescant's head floating in clouds, to Palissy ware in high polychrome relief, to a romanesque carved chessman.

Immediately next to the Founders' Room, in a small gallery, it is hoped to mount a new display of more Tradescant and other early material. Maybe Guy Fawkes's lantern, which is probably the object that children prefer amongst all others in the whole Museum, even above the Alfred Jewel and the model of Pliny's villa, will end up here. (The lantern was not Tradescant's, but given to the University by the son of one of Fawkes's apprehenders, in 1641.) This display will include the skin-cloak of

Egyptian Limestone: *Pharaoh Khasekhem*. Second dynasty, *c.* 2800 B.C.

Pocahontas's father, exhibited at the time of writing outside the Heberden Coin Room door. Marvellous misch-masch; another specimen of American Indian *haute couture*, a deer-skin hunting shirt, claimed to be the oldest surviving. Chinese boots, a buddha, a crossbow, Henry VIII's stirrups. Perhaps to be kept with these are other celebrated objects of sentimental associational value, several transferred from their original homes in the Bodleian—like the iron-lined hat (or safety helmet) worn by John Bradshaw when presiding over the court that condemned Charles I in 1649 (an occupation that Bradshaw no doubt considered to have its dangers). The hat was given in 1715. Likewise of not very cosy iron, a cradle said to have belonged to Henry VI, and the earliest surviving University Chest, dated 1411, or 1426, lent by Corpus Christi College.

These are objects connected with the early history of the Museum. Memorials of a far remoter antiquity are housed in one room, the Drapers' Gallery, which is to be found somewhat inconsequentially in the northeastern extremity of the first floor. It is a space that holds in its small confine the fragmentary history of what I still think of as the beginnings of western civilisation (despite all evidence to the contrary from such earlier sites as the caves at Lascaux, Les Eyzies, or Altamira): the cultures of the Near East, of Palestine, the Lebanon; of Syria, Iraq, Jordan and Persia. The depth of time plotted by the objects in these calm and shining cases is difficult to grasp for those not used to daily traffic with antiquity. Yet here you will find one of a group of heads (from Kathleen Kenyon's digs at Jericho in the nineteen-fifties) that are arguably the earliest portraits in the world: this is a skull, clad with a kind of plaster. An individual head of perhaps nine to ten thousand years ago, metamorphosed into something rich and strange, its eyes not pearls but sea-shells—and yet modern anthropologists have brought back heads even of our own century that are almost indistinguishable from these, plastered skulls with cowrie eyes, from New Guinea. The exhibits in the Drapers' Gallery range from this beginning till round the time of Christ, and the area they cover reaches from the Mediterranean shores of Turkey or the Red Sea almost as far as Afghanistan: the area long celebrated as the cradle of the three great religions of the West, and where written language begins. Here, the "Weld-Blundell" Prism is pre-eminent. It is one of the oldest historical texts, written in cuneiform script and listing in sequence, from times before the Flood, the rollcall of Sinerian kings. It dates from about 1800 B.C. Much later, there is an example of the jars and linen wrappings that held the celebrated and controversial Dead Sea Scrolls, hidden by monks of the monastery at Qumran threatened by Roman troops about A.D. 66. There are also the beginnings of glass manufacture—the Tell Atshana vessel (*c.*1400–1300 B.C.) made by coiling molten glass. Much of this display is primarily of archaeological and historical importance,

Egyptian Bronze (with gold earrings, perhaps modern): *Cat, sacred to the goddess Bastet.* Late period, *c.* 1075–333 B.C.

often witness to a remarkable series of scientifically controlled excavations, many by famous pioneer archaeologists with close links to Oxford, like Sir Leonard Woolley, Sir Flinders Petrie, T. E. Lawrence and many others. They also include many objects that are striking in their own right: a notable and rich representation of the Luristan bronzes, mostly horse-furniture, from western Iran around 1000 B.C. onwards; the big Assyrian relief, characteristic profile of those impressive if unamicable eagle-headed winged figures from a palace at Nimrod, about the ninth century B.C.; or the vivid little ivory plaque of a winged sphinx also from Nimrod though made in Phoenicia about 300–700 B.C. (It has been suggested that the cherubim of Solomon's temple would have looked like much larger elder brothers of this image.) There is also gold jewellery, but pottery is preponderant, ranging from ordinary domestic ware to those humped open-mouthed Amlash bull vases or pitchers from northern Iran, about 1200 B.C. To the modern eye accustomed to contemporary art these may seem comfortably and charmingly kin to, say, certain sculptures or ceramics by Picasso.

Reversing through the Antiquities' galleries from this beginning, you can trace the development of western and near-

LEFT: Human skull, plastered and painted with cowrie eyes. From a Pre-Pottery Neolithic 'B' settlement (*c.* 7500–7000 B.C.) at Jericho.

RIGHT: Assyrian marble relief: *Eagle-headed winged figure*. From the Northwest palace at Nimrod, ninth century B.C.

TOP LEFT: Cypro-archaic, bichrome IV barrel-jug *c.* 700–600 B.C.

TOP RIGHT: Cypro-archaic limestone: *Head of a Bearded Man.* Fourth century B.C.

Greek pelike from Rhodes. Attic black-figure painting, *A Shoemaker*, by the Eucharides painter. Fifth century B.C.

eastern civilisation. Nearby is the crowded display of Cypriot material civilisation. Movements from the Near East, Asia Minor and Greece pervaded Cyprus—inevitably, the island being sited where it is—and these are reflected in the styles and decoration of Cypriot pottery and in the sculpture: the admirable limestone head of the close, curly-bearded man with the slight and faintly sinister smile seems to reflect both East and West. This is the richest display of Cypriot wares and art outside Cyprus, as that of the pre-historic Aegean that leads on from it (Arthur Evans Room) is in some aspects the most comprehensive outside Crete. This of course results from Arthur Evans's activities in Crete (for Evans see p. 30), themselves nostalgic reminders of ampler times when archaeologists seemed often to be men of means as well as of devouring curiosity and energy, prepared to set about the hidden resources of the past with both science and abandon. When Evans became interested in the legendary palace of Knossos, he simply bought it. As an archaeologist of conscience and responsibility, most of the finds, and all but all the big ones, he left naturally in Greek hands; but the wealth of small objects that came out of Crete—fragments of frescoes, Linear B tablets, bronze tools and weapons, painted pottery of the Old and New Palace periods—must make a modern archaeologist sigh with envy. In fact now, as is only proper, the proprietary countries of

Cretan clay-tablet showing linear B inscription recording chariot wheels. From Knossos, *c.* 1400 B.C.

archaeological sites are gradually closing down all distribution of archaeological finds to other countries, even to those foreign excavators who are active on the sites. Smuggling is of course notoriously rife, but the gradual cessation of growth by the relevant great collections of the world, like the Ashmolean's, will not stop smuggling as long as private collectors the world over are prepared to pay high prices for objects that are too "hot" for responsible museums to consider. The problem was already there in Evans's time, but in nothing like so prohibitive a form.

Especially noteworthy here and throughout the early near-Eastern, Aegean and Greek collections, is an enormous almost inexhaustible wealth of seal-stones and cylinder seals. These sound boring, but constitute in fact a wonderful treasury of the history of artistic forms in the region, which can now—thanks to the efficiency of modern photography—be made available to the general public. From the islands of the Cyclades, there is a remarkably fine series of those doll-like, potently blank yet saturnine marble votive statuettes of the early Bronze Age, now so much admired (and so much forged).

The collection of pre-historic witness from Europe is housed in a room named after John Evans, and his collections are still richly represented there. The range is probably more comprehensive than anywhere in Britain except the British Museum.

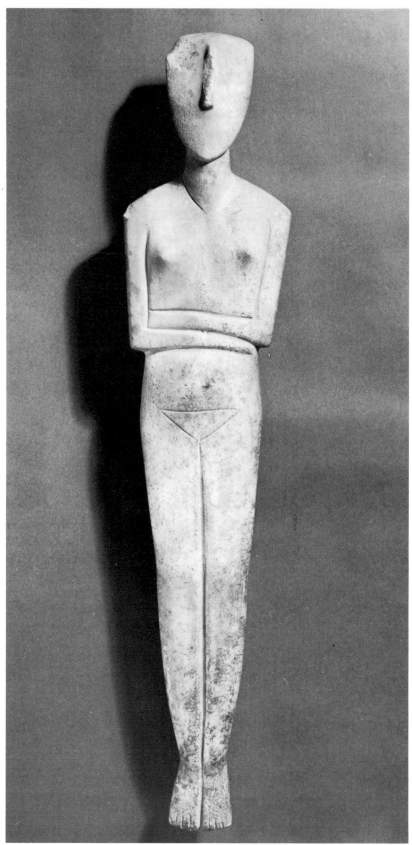

Modern impressions of Cretan sealstones.
From Minoan sites, second millennium B.C.

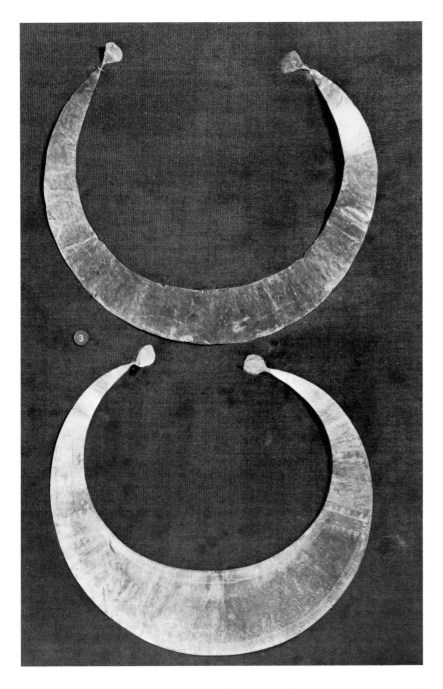

Two Irish gold lumulae, perhaps used as neck ornaments. Early Bronze Age (early to middle second millennium B.C.).

Thus there is West Russian Tripolye Culture pottery (3rd millennium B.C.); objects from Spain, France, the Balkans, Germany and Scandinavia; Thracian silver, and gold torcs from various sources. The British representation is naturally rich in local finds, of Beaker Culture objects especially, and the contents of a young man's grave at Radley—just down the road—of the early 2nd millennium B.C. The strange geometry of prehistoric sites, invisible on the ground but shining clearly through the deciduous surface of the modern landscape to the eye of the air-borne camera is generously shown in a sequence of photographs

OPPOSITE: Greek marble idol, from Amorgos (Cyclades). Early third millennium B.C.

39

Greek cup from Chiusi. The painting, *Boy with Hoop*, is by the "Colmar" painter. Attic, *c.* 500 B.C. Detail.

OPPOSITE: *Head of Demosthenes*, Roman copy of a lost Bronze statue by Polyeuktos, 280 B.C.

by the pioneer aerial photographer, G. W. G. Allen: the Museum holds his entire collection.

Greece is of course very comprehensively represented, and the fantastically rich coverage of Greek vases is especially associated with the great Oxford scholar Sir John Beazley. One pretty example reproduced here, the timeless boy in such elegant control of his hoop some 2,400 years ago (by the Colmar painter, *c.* 500 B.C.) can indicate something of the quality attained by the case painters and potters. This is just one item shown in the Ashmolean display of the development of Greek vase-painting. In something of a departure from old practice, the revised, much thinned display (made possible by the generous von Bothmer benefaction) in the Ashmolean gives room for the best of the pots to breathe: each is isolated so that the eye can concentrate on it undisturbed, and yet the whole is set out in chronological sequence, and matched step-by-step with comparative examples of terracotta modelling and other arts.

Rome, pre-Roman Italy and the Roman Empire are

concentrated in the John Evans Room. Here is Etruria, that rich and independent culture that flourished from the 8th century B.C. until it was submerged by Rome—though long before that it had been infiltrated by Hellenistic inspiration or actual imports from Greece. Thus in this context too the art of the Greek vase is represented (and some fine examples of Etruscan provenance appear in the main Greek display as well, for they were imports though found in Etruria). The gold and bronze objects illustrate especially the striking individuality of the Etruscan character: the statuette of Turms, early 5th century; an admirable seated lion; or a fine example of those small statuettes of Umbrian warriors, shrunk to a Giacommetti-like thinness.

The huge spread of Roman culture ramified through Europe, Egypt, Asia Minor, North Africa; in the Ashmolean it is brought together in one area (Leeds Room). Oil lamps, terracotta

Roman bronze, inlaid with silver: *Dancing Lar* c. first century A.D.

or bronze; bronze figures continuing the Greek tradition—often coarsely, but some pieces are of high quality: the little dancing Lar, of perhaps the 1st century A.D. (the first contribution of the Friends of the Ashmolean after their foundation in 1970), or the firmly and massively modelled Cupid found at Cirencester. Glass of all kinds, but now almost all blown (and mostly fetchingly devitrified by time, and so acquiring that milky almost fluorescent quality). Towards the close of the period the classical tradition disintegrates before your eyes into the Dark Ages: Saxon grave goods, and a rare collection of brooches and jewellery with that rich interlace decoration once classified as barbaric.

Also in the Leeds Room are examples of that most vivid Egypto-Roman amalgam—the brilliant painted mummy faces, dating from the first to fourth century A.D., from the Fayoum area. The development of the main Egyptian tradition, from

OPPOSITE LEFT: Umbrian bronze statuette of a warrior. Fifth century B.C.

OPPOSITE: Roman marble bust, life-size: *The Emperor Lucius Verus* (A.D. 161–69). From Probalinthos near Marathon, late second century A.D.

Roman bull of pipeclay terracotta. From Amiens, second century A.D.

4000 B.C. on—of which these faces, so immediate, almost contemporary, with their exaggerated wide and staring eyes, are the conclusion—is displayed in the big galleries on the ground floor. These also house the larger pieces of classical statuary—mainly Roman, but a few Greek, and a great deal of it originating in the Arundel collection, though some of the finest pieces came from other sources. These include, most recently, yet another gift from a member of the Evans family, this time Dame Joan Evans, the half-sister of Sir Arthur; a delicate and tender marble head, Hellenistic, of Hermes Psychopompos. Later are two tall elaborate candelabra from Hadrian's villa at Tivoli, which were owned and restored by Piranesi.

The Egyptian collections are housed in some density. The Petrie Room, pre-dynastic objects and mostly from Sir Flinders Petrie's excavations; the Chester Room, writing materials, the *shawabtis* mentioned above, seals, scarabs, amulets, jewelry; the Egyptian Dynastic Gallery, packed with small finds

ABOVE: The Stanton Cross. From Ixworth, Suffolk, *c*. A.D. 650.

BRONZE FIGURE OF CUPID.
PLOUGHED UP AT A SPOT CALLED "THE LEWSES"
CIRENCESTER IN 1752. AT THE SAME PLACE A ROMAN
HYPOCAUST WAS SUBSEQUENTLY DISCOVERED. THE
FIGURE IS FINELY MODELLED AND BOTH FOR SIZE AND
WORKMANSHIP RANKS AMONG THE FIRST SPECIMENS OF
GRAECO-ROMAN ART FOUND IN BRITAIN. THE EYE-SOCKETS
ARE OF SILVER AND THERE ARE HOLES IN THE SHOUL-
DERS FOR THE ATTACHMENT OF WINGS.
ARCHAEOLOGIA VI. 1.03]

LEFT: Roman bronze Cupid. From
Cirencester, second century A.D.

45

from excavated sites; and the Griffith Gallery, where larger pieces, including the whole shrine of Pharaoh Taharqa (*c.*691–666 B.C.) —carved reliefs, statues, fragments of wall paintings, mummies, all lit by artificial light in a forced brilliance that emphasises the surreal clarity of this culture of the tomb. The collections are specially valuable in that they are mostly from controlled and documented excavations, which got under way mainly from the second half of the nineteenth century. Not all, however: *shawabtis* were given to the University by Archbishop Laud before 1635 (and even at that early date, one was already a forgery); a fine relief from a false door from Saqqara came from the Rev. Robert Huntington in 1683. The Egyptian collections are another favourite with children. They are excitingly spooky—the polychrome, wide-eyed brilliance of mummy-cases creating their own silence—but also packed with vivid detail like a toy-shop window. Although the evidence of Egyptian daily life that survives comes mostly out of tombs, the Egyptians believed that they needed, in the after-life, a complete equipment for ordinary life as they had known it. Hence the cosmetic apparatus; those touching dolls-house scale models of people, boats—a granary for example, with a scribe recording output; writing materials, jewels, tools—and of course the ever-macabre presence of the bodies themselves, preserved through tens of centuries, and their integuments, the layers of their carved and painted containers.

"Antiquities" at the Ashmolean extends in fact for some categories through the Middle Ages to as late as the seventeenth century. Almost unnervingly close to Egypt are the Mediaeval Room and, beyond that (in the Library Lobby at the front of the northwest stairs), the display of Viking material. The Mediaeval Room is a small space with a packed display: pottery, especially local, sculpture, keys, spurs, seals; watches of Oxford provenance (Oxford is rich for watch-fanciers, for they appear also in the Department of Western Art, and then again in the Museum of the History of Science). But the hub about which all this revolves is that one magic object, the Alfred Jewel.

CHAPTER FOUR

THE ASHMOLEAN MUSEUM

Department of Western Art

INTO THE DEPARTMENT OF Western Art, a considerable number of elements have gradually come together. As a gallery of art its history begins with the Bodleian Gallery, to which gifts of paintings came early in the history of the Bodleian Library, and which was the oldest public picture-gallery in England. Thus several of the Dutch pictures left by the Rev. John King in 1739 are still identifiable, and cherished. A major stage in the consolidation of the University's paintings came with the building of the University Galleries (the present Ashmolean building) in 1845 and the transfer of the Bodleian paintings to them: when the collections under the Ashmolean roof finally took the common title of Ashmolean in 1908, the paintings, drawings and prints, together with the objects classified as "decorative" or "applied" art, were assigned to the Department of Fine Art within the Ashmolean. A final clarification came in 1961 with the establishment of the Department of Eastern Art, whereupon the Department of Fine Art became the Department of Western Art (transferring its holdings of Persian and Turkish ceramics to its newborn neighbour).

The beginnings of the united collections in their new home in 1845 were saluted in the following year by an endowment that now seems almost fabulous, the Lawrence/Woodburn collection of drawings by Michelangelo and Raphael and related artists. In the inevitable winnowing of the scientific art-historical appraisal of later generations, the number of drawings firmly attributable to these two masters' own hands may have shrunk, but the interest and beauty of the drawings remain unimpaired. (It is sometimes forgotten that while art-historians and curators proceed upon their checking and counter-checking, labelling and re-labelling with different names, the objects themselves remain

ABOVE LEFT: Rembrandt van Rijn: *Saskia Asleep in Bed*. Pen and brush drawing, 1635.

ABOVE: Michelangelo: *Studies for the Sistine Ceiling and the Tomb of Julius II*. Red chalk and pen with brown ink, *c*. 1512/13.

unchanged.) There is no argument but that the collection of Raphael drawings is amongst the two or three richest collections of his graphic work in the world—and arguably, it is the finest. It is composed not only of those first thoughts and doodles that rightly entrance art-historians, but also of marvellously wrought drawings that stop the non-specialists too in their tracks. The famous drawing by Raphael long held to be of himself aged about fifteen is probably not a self-portrait but it is just what the boy in the budding of genius ought to have looked like; the study of the heads and hands of St. John and St. Peter (studies for the *Transfiguration*, *c*. 1519–20) is startlingly vivid and equally famous.

The source of these drawings was Sir Thomas Lawrence, P.R.A., remembered not only as the brilliant portrait painter of the Regency, but also as a voracious collector of Old Master drawings. At his death in 1830, he left instructions that his collection be offered, at a price far below its true value, to the Crown—and then, if the offer was not taken, to the British Museum and others. None of those named rose to the occasion, and the collection was gradually dispersed for sale by the Woodburns, dealers through whom Lawrence had mainly worked when forming it. Samuel Woodburn, however, was determined that the most important section—consisting of Raphael and Michelangelo—should both be kept together, and remain in the country. Seven thousand pounds was in question (for drawings now worth millions), but even that modest sum proved difficult, and it took the generosity of John, 2nd Earl of Eldon, to save the day with a single contribution of £4,000.

The range and richness of the collection of drawings has been built up in the Ashmolean Print Room since Lawrence's days. That first deposit proved a magnet to attract further gifts of now astonishing rarity and value, notably the 1st Earl of Ellesmere's

OPPOSITE: Raphael: *Studies of two Apostles*. Black chalk drawing touched with white.

Rembrandt van Rijn: *The Artist's Studio.*
Pen and ink, wash touched with body-
colour.

OPPOSITE: Francesco Guardi: *Venice: the Ponte di Rialto.* Pen and grey wash.

(in 1853) and that of Chambers Hall (1855). The Ellesmere gift was of sixty-eight drawings by the Carracci—Lodovico, Agostino and Annibale—and artists close to them. This was a particularly happy reunion, as they too had come from Lawrence's collection. Chambers Hall's benefaction included drawings by or attributed to Leonardo da Vinci (5), Correggio (6), Dürer (4), Rembrandt (19), A. van Ostade (27), and Claude le Lorrain (30). A few years later, in 1863, a general body was given to the collection as an entity by the transfer to the University Galleries of the drawings that had come to the Bodleian, along with books and manuscripts, in the enormously rich bequest of Francis Douce (1834). The Douce bequest included early Italian drawings connected with artists as various as Botticelli, Campagnola, Filippo Lippi, Pisanello, and as late as the Venetians, Pittoni or G. B. Tiepolo. It also contained wonderful German and Dutch drawings—among them the famous Grünewald of the woman with clasped hands, and works by Altdorfer, Schöngauer, Holbein the Younger, Baldung-Grien; then Watteau drawings, Van Dyck, and so on, while the English drawings held a cross-section of seventeenth- and eighteenth-century work, including an admirable selection of Rowlandsons with an unimpeachable pedigree, as they were bought by Douce direct from the artist.

Giovanni Batista Piazzetta:
Head of a Youth. Black and white chalks.

OPPOSITE: "Mathias Grünewald": *Elderly
Woman with Clasped Hands*. Charcoal
drawing.

The wealth that has built on these beginnings, to make the Ashmolean collection one of the most remarkable in the world, can hardly even be indicated here. The originals of the picturesque prints that adorn the annual Oxford Almanacks, the sequence of views of Oxford, continuous from the eighteenth century, have been deposited by the Clarendon Press. It includes work by Turner, Dayes, de Wint, Muirhead Bone, and the tradition continues today. The stock of Turners was supplemented liberally by John Ruskin, and many other donors have built up the holding of works of the English watercolour school—a branch of art practised in Britain with a felicity and originality unmatched elsewhere: the Cozens, Girtin, David Cox, Cotman and so up to Wilson Steer and beyond, all are well represented. Whilst the Blake drawings may not be comparable with the Fitzwilliam collection at Cambridge, the Ashmolean has become the mecca for all who love the work of Samuel Palmer, especially the mystic visions of the few years of his Shoreham period in the 1820s. Palmer provokes an extraordinary direct response from a very wide section of the public, including people who may be rather baffled by Raphael or Michelangelo. I admit happily to this Palmer compulsion, and find it difficult to pass the Palmer drawings without stopping; hence, as the selection of illustrations must

Samuel Palmer: *Self-Portrait*. Black chalks heightened with white.

Samuel Palmer: *The Valley with a Bright Cloud*. Pen and brush in sepia, 1825.

OPPOSITE: Antoine Watteau: *A Girl Seated with Music in her Lap*. Red, black, and white chalks.

necessarily be fairly arbitrary, I include with no apology two of his most famous works.

Print rooms in most museums are maddeningly frustrating and the Ashmolean is no exception, though its tradition of service will never, I hope, grow less. For reasons of space they can never show more than a fraction of their treasures framed on a wall; nor, even were there space enough and time, could they do so, as prolonged exposure to light destroys. The Ashmolean normally has a selection of the drawings, changing every month or so, hung in the Eldon Gallery, or occasionally also in the McAlpine Gallery. It also has permanently a selection of Samuel Palmers and another of that other, very different Oxford speciality, the tiny-toed attenuated caricatures of Max Beerbohm, on public exhibition. These cause complaint because they are shown in a very low light (to avoid harming them), but such is the public demand to see them that they might suffer ruin by being hauled out of cases daily.

The ordinary visitor who wants to test and savour the range of the Ashmolean drawings needs to do a little homework on the catalogue first, so that he may know what he wants to ask to see. The catalogues of drawings published by the Museum are fortunately admirable—begun by a former Keeper, Sir Karl Parker, an outstanding scholar of old master drawings, who by his flair for acquisitions consolidated the heterogeneous collections into a representative holding of the work of most schools and periods. Unhappily, the catalogue of British drawings has still to be realised.

The Print Room also contains the Museum's collection of engravings. These have been acquired by degrees, like the drawings. The basis of the old master series is from the Douce collection, with its numerous fifteenth-century woodcuts— many unique—and fifteenth- and seventeenth-century engravings: Dürer, Altdorfer, Cranach, Pollaiuolo, Mantegna, and so forth. Aptly in context with the Raphael drawings, the early Raphaelesque engraver, Marcantonio Raimondi, and comparable Italians, are represented in depth. There are etchings by Carracci, Barocci, Salvator Rosa, and the great sequences of etchings by Rembrandt (claimed as one of the finest in the world), by Van Dyck, Ostade, and Claude—all these come from Chambers Hall. Turner is represented notably by the full *Liber Studiorum* (many of these etchings in more than one state). The Museum's connection with the Pissarro family is reflected in a rich holding of prints and drawings, especially by Camille Pissarro. In addition the Print Room houses a class of prints that tends to be of more documentary than artistic interest—a huge archive of portrait and topographical prints, the Hope collection and the Sutherland collection. These represent a combination which is scarcely paralleled anywhere else, and include many unique items: the portrait engraving archive is surpassed only by those in the

National Portrait Gallery (for British subjects) and the British Museum.

It may be that I seem to have given over much attention to drawings and prints. But they are the richest, most important holding of the Department of Western Art; they are also the section of the Department which needs most introduction, as it cannot be seen, nor its importance guessed at, by the casual visitor to the main exhibition galleries. The paintings in Western Art provide a somewhat less comprehensive illustration of the main streams in the history of European art than that offered by the drawings. Even so, they do afford the visitor with a range of paintings of high, sometimes superb quality, of international rather than merely national stature.

The first signs of major growth in the then new University Galleries were provided in 1850 by William Fox-Strangways (later 4th Earl of Ilchester), whom we shall encounter later as a major benefactor of paintings to Christ Church. Fox-Strangways, though not the first Englishman to collect Italian pictures of before 1500 (those that used to be called "primitives"), was an early and ardent admirer of them. He bought copiously and then, with equally copious generosity, bestowed his acquisitions upon Oxford. The pattern of growth has since been conditioned by an irregular but extraordinarily rich sequence of benefactions. In spite of what, in comparison with American practices, can only seem to potential benefactors a national fiscal system designed to discourage those who wish to encourage museums and galleries, this practice is still far from extinct. In the last decades, with the growth in the Department of modest trust funds and a variable but always welcome contribution to the Museum purchasing funds from the University's central resources, it has proved possible to build up the collections rather more systematically than is usual in the random pattern of benefaction—so glorious but so unpredictable, and dependent on private collectors' tastes. Sir Karl Parker's Keepership (1934–62) was scarcely less remarkable for the growth by purchase in paintings and in works of the applied and decorative arts than it was in drawings. His successors have continued to deploy restricted funds to maximum effect. They have received invaluable support from outside sources, especially the National Art-Collections Fund, and the grant allocated by the Government to the Victoria and Albert Museum for purchases by provincial museums.

The Western Art galleries are on the upper floors. Access is by the chaste, gravely austere main staircase that ascends from right of the Museum's entrance. Those accustomed to lifts may pause in the ascent at the landing to encourage their aspiration with a sight of the cast of the Bassae frieze, men and centaurs for ever in conflict around the top of the stairwell under the cool light of the central lantern.

The first room at the top has been (since 1949) the

Founders' Lobby, devoted to the Tradescant and Ashmole portraits (which we have already glimpsed, p. 28), and showcases with small magic bric-à-brac from the Tradescant collections. Thence the galleries evolve, not in large ordered progress as in, say, the Fitzwilliam at Cambridge, but by a leading-on that can seem almost mazy, an alternation of larger and smaller spaces offering sudden and unexpected pleasures of discovery. The nucleus of the earlier Italian paintings still resides in the Fox-Strangways gift. Works by the hands of, say, Cimabue, Giotto or Duccio may be lacking but there are pictures of very remarkable quality by their followers in the fourteenth century. The Orcagna *Birth of the Virgin* is a vision of both majesty and tenderness, very substantial within one of those fragile pavilions, so characteristic of the school, pitched with such artifice on a gold eternity. Or the combined *Crucifixion* and *Lamentation* by Barna da Siena, the agony and frenzy of grief encompassed in the eloquent stylisation of the crouching, draped mourners. In a lighter, almost rollicking mood, Bicci de Lorenzo's *St Nicholas rebuking the Tempest*, one of the most popular paintings in the Museum: the airborne saint planing in over the tattered sails of the rounded, rocking ship, bringing clear skies and a galaxy of stars as he routs the storm. That is from a later date, however, as is the most famous and enchanting of Fox-Strangways' gift, Uccello's famous *Hunt in the Forest*, painted by the artist late in his long life (about 1460). While it has all of Uccello's passionate delight in perspective and strange symmetries, it seems to me the most humane of his work that has survived, and also one of the most romantic works of the whole fifteenth century. It is that strange thing—apart from being a night piece, the sickle moon over the dark trees stained with thin mist—a picture in which everyone is receding at top speed from the spectator. Physiognomical expression is through profiles, and if you look long enough, you may hear the echo of the clamour of those open mouths in the forest or the bray of the up-raised horn. The movement is quick, vital, yet frozen: as though the dance to the music of time had been stopped in full career.

The Uccello was perhaps a *cassone* panel. It has been suggested it represents the young Lorenzo de Medici hunting near Pisa. You can inform slightly your guess on that from the superb terracotta, based on the death mask of Lorenzo, that stands on a bracket next to the painting, matched with one of the contemporary versions of Daniel da Volterra's bronze of Michelangelo's head, likewise said (by Vasari) to be based on a death-mask. A worthy counterpart to the Uccello is the almost equally dream-intense—indeed surreal—vision of Piero di Cosimo's *Forest Fire*, with its panic rout of animals and birds (some lumbering ominously through the air as if heavy with bombs), all the more disquieting because some of the animals that turn to look at you have human faces. Amongst the portraits proper, the characteristic clarity of a Ghirlandaio *Young Man* in fez-like hat, his identity long lost as he too is lost in sideways reverie; from a later date, the princely presence in ornate frame of another Medici—the boy *Don Garzia de' Medici* by the Mannerist prince of court painters, Bronzino.

Usually shown in context with these and the other early Italians are the Renaissance bronzes. These are a formidable collection, largely from C. D. E. Fortnum (1820–99). Fortnum is sometimes called the second Founder of the Museum—a title due no less to him than to his close ally and collaborator, Sir Arthur Evans. Fortnum had those admirable characteristics that seemed to cohabit in one person more frequently in Victorian times than now—wealth, insatiable curiosity, acquisitiveness, high and, if need be, ruthless altruism, taste, discrimination, and learning. He started as a scientist, and when he turned to art it was from a scientific angle; thus through the study of the technology and manufacturing processes and sites of early Italian pottery, he became for a time the foremost authority on the subject, especially on majolica. This interest extended, through an interest in the techniques of casting, to bronzes, and those now in the Ashmolean are a remarkable range. (The cases in which many of them are shown are museum-pieces in their own right: Egyptian green porphyry on mahogany, from that famous neo-classical house, Thomas Hope's *Deepdene*, and made for it; and rosewood and red porphyry from the famous state drawing-room at Stowe and of about the same period.) The best known and indeed most seductive of individual pieces is by one of the greatest makers of bronzes, Andrea Riccio, a marvellous alert and sensitive version of his seated *Pan listening to Echo*. Bronzes of all kinds and often by the major practitioners are generously represented—Florentine, Paduan, Venetian. There are some romanesque examples and several very fine Flemish, German, and Viennese. Subjects, apart from figures, include ink stands, door-knockers, salt-cellars. Later bronzes and small sculptures are displayed here and there through the galleries, while the very fine collection of bronze plaquettes (many from Fortnum's collection) are at present in cases alongside the displays of plate, as also the medals. The latter (many of the finest from the Douce bequest, transferred from the Bodleian) include a magisterial representation of those wonderfully economical but massive profiles by the first Italian master of medals, Pisanello.

Majolica, another of the categories introduced by the Fortnum benefaction, is a medium that attracts passionate advocates but also physically repels others, especially those dishes with renderings in violent polychrome of Raphaelesque encounters of saints or divinities or mythological heroes or tales from Aesop. But some forms of majolica—essentially an enamelling with oxide of tin—are irresistible to most people. Such are the Spanish-Moresque wares, in vivid blues and metallic lustres:

Andrea Riccio: *Pan listening to Echo*.
Bronze.

OPPOSITE: Pellegrino Tibaldi (?) or Giovanni
Demio: *Adoration of the Shepherds*. Panel,
c. 1550–60(?).

massive dishes that it seems sinful not to load with the teeming ripe fruit of the Mediterranean. Majolica in all its forms delighted Fortnum, and the representation in the Museum is consequently rich: Deruta, Gubbio, Urbino, Castel Durante, Faenza, Pesaro— most of the famous centres, and many of the best masters. In this context, look especially for the little Medici porcelain ewer of 1580, from the Grand Duke's experimental factory at Florence: perhaps the earliest porcelain made in Europe and one of the most coveted of all ceramic rarities.

Among the Italian pictures, those of the sixteenth century are shown mainly in the small Italian Room. Apart from the elegant enchantment of the Mannerist *Adoration of the Shepherds* by Pellegrino Tibaldi(?), serene and rapt in the early light, set in the ruins of a classical temple, the paintings are mostly Venetian. Two beautiful paintings, by great names—Bellini, the last of the old, and Giorgione, the first of the new—sway in and out of the art-historian's accepted canon of works actually by the masters. At the time of writing, both seem to be in, but their quality always has been of the highest, and is undimmed by their theoretical mutations. Bellini's *St Jerome*, a small panel: the elderly saint seated outside his niche turning his book, his lion placidly domestic —and beyond, the clear-cut grouping of a village and the foothills of north Italy receding in radiance to the horizon. The Giorgione:

a composed young Madonna, marvellously complete in her composure, reading (certainly the Good Book) to an infant Christ almost aggressively alert in his precocious attention, with the Doge's palace at Venice building beyond—a strange poetic amalgam of supernatural and matter-of-fact that seems to me entirely consonant, though different in theme, with the more famous handful of Giorgione's masterpieces. Then there is Tintoretto, an *Ascension of Christ*, with the Saviour positively exploding heavenwards from an intolerable constraint of the tomb and of his followers. Jacopo Bassano, Montagna, Veronese. Then from Urbino, Barocci's *St Dominic de Guzman receiving the Rosary* which in the fluency, the heady exaltation and sweetness of its fervour, looks forward to the seventeenth century.

The strength of that century is concentrated especially in two noble works of Italianate Frenchmen. The fine *Exposition of Moses* by Nicholas Poussin, with all that characteristic distancing of human grief (or joy) in a classical landscape, and the supremely romantic *Ascanius shooting the Stag*, the last picture that Claude Lorrain painted, in the last year of his life (1682); seeming about to dissolve indeed into a blue dusk, with a storm threatening, but with no trace of any hesitation in the touch of one of the greatest manipulators of time and distance who ever painted. The great baroque "machines" of *seicento* painting are not represented but there are excellent smaller works by artists such as Annibale Carracci, Mola, Vouet, Strozzi and Solimena, while from the eighteenth century a tiny Watteau, and some very fine Venetian examples. A magnificent, crowded unusual Guardi of a *Papal Blessing: Campo SS. Giovanni e Paolo*; and an (again unusual) endlessly popular and pretty Tiepolo of a *Girl with a Macaw*. The Weldon Gallery itself is perhaps the most gently elegant in the Museum—furnished with fine French furniture, with delicate table cases containing delicate portrait miniatures (not the Museum's greatest strength, but with very fine eighteenth-century representation) and snuff boxes: there are bronzes and freely-moulded *bozzetti* in terracotta.

There is no space here unfortunately to stray in detail, from item to item, through the remaining galleries. Thus the little Pre-Raphaelite Room with the collection bequeathed by the Combe family who bought from Holman Hunt, Millais and others very early in their careers, can only be glanced at. The young of today tend to linger there, and eyes brought up in the normalities of strident colour provided by schools such as the Abstract Expressionists, have no difficulty in accepting the colour clashes of Holman Hunt—nor, apparently, the bombardment of his sentiment. Arthur Hughes's *Home from the Sea* is quieter in feeling, and indeed one of the most touching of all Pre-Raphaelite paintings. Inchbold's landscape (though Inchbold was not actually a member of the Brotherhood) is admirable illustration of the movement's insistence on the direct approach; an image that can

OPPOSITE: Federigo Barocci: *St. Dominic Receiving the Rosary*. Oils on paper, *c.* 1588.

63

John William Inchbold: *In Early Spring*.
Canvas.

remind one in middle-age of the immediacy, the endless possibili-
ties, of youth. Of the continental nineteenth century there is
ample evidence—Pissarro particularly, owing to the family's
(and especially Orovida Pissarro's) affectionate and generous
connection with the Ashmolean. Toulouse-Lautrec is here (*La
Toilette*); and a typical van Gogh pre-Provence colouristic essay,
Restaurant de la Sirène Asnières—evidence of continuing benefaction, for it was bequeathed in 1973. These are supported by
good examples of pre-Impressionist giants—Corot, Courbet—
while there is also an unexpected, uncharacteristic, and utterly
charming Picasso of blue roofs. The English twentieth-century

OPPOSITE: Giovanni Battista Tiepolo: *A
Young Woman with a Macaw*. Canvas.

Vincent van Gogh: *Restaurant de la Sirène,*
Asnières. Oil on canvas, 1886/7.

representation is confined mainly to traditional figurative painting
—excellent examples of Camden Town painting—Sickert,
Gore, Gilman, and Bevan. Experimental art is the province of
Oxford's Museum of Modern Art; on the other hand, part of the
most recent increase of space in the Ashmolean Museum, the
gallery so generously given by Mr. and Mrs. Alistair McAlpine, is
specifically intended for loan exhibitions of contemporary art.

As for the applied arts, there is a great luxury: the majolica;
the examples of Renaissance sculpture; Limoges enamels; the
large collection of finger rings of all periods; the internationally
important collection of watches; the superb collection of plate,
especially of Huguenot silver, with a whole caseful of the work
of the most famous of all Huguenot silversmiths, Paul de Lamerie.
In a small room, in built-in cases, a delightful and domestically
cosy display of English Delft pottery. There is also, though in a
sort of appendix-room (outside the Coin Room entrance, and

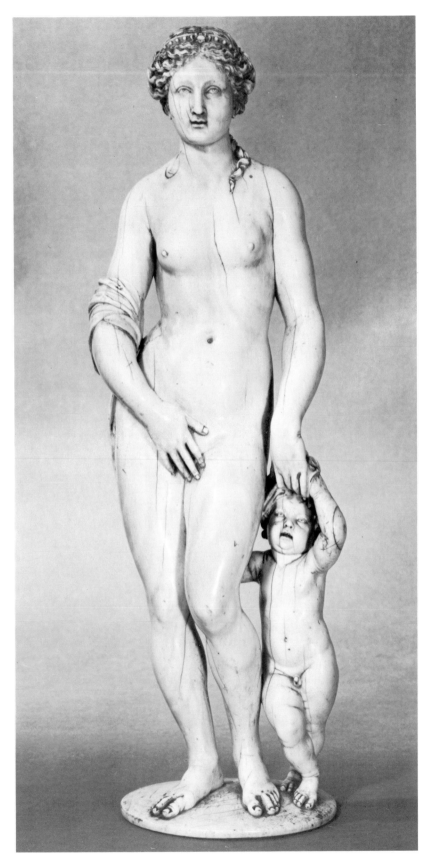

LEFT: Georg Petel: *Venus and Cupid*. Ivory.

BELOW: Genoese silver basin and ewer, made for the Lomellini family, 1619.

BOTTOM: George Smith: Watch in a gold pomander case, *c.* 1600. The watch is said to have belonged to Queen Elizabeth I.

Antonio Stradivari: Violin "Le Messie".
1716.

easily missable) the Hill collection of musical instruments, mainly stringed and by London or Italian makers, notably of Brescia and Cremona. Amongst them there is a late seventeenth-century spinet with charming painted decoration of ladies and gentlemen in pastoral badinage. But above all, perhaps the most famous Stradivarius violin in the world, known as "Le Messie" with its original label visible through the f-holes: "*Antonius Stradiuarius Cremonensis Faciebat Anne 1716*".

In the Tapestry Gallery there is a central hush, in spite of its use as junction on this floor, of great tapestries, with sculpture. *Christopher Wren*, by Pierce, is at once the finest English baroque bust by an English sculptor and the only adequate rendering of the physical personality of the greatest of English architects in his springtime. Also in slightly rum contrast are the somewhat dour

ABOVE LEFT: Franco-Flemish school: *Pieta*. Panel, *c.* 1480(?).

ABOVE: Edward Pierce: *Sir Christopher Wren*. Marble, *c.* 1670(?).

69

John Constable: *Watermeadows near Salisbury*. Canvas, *c.* 1820/21.

presences of Oliver Cromwell, by Pierce, and of the great soldier, Marlborough, by Rysbrack. In this gallery the light is subdued. Candelabra. Baroque papal busts. On great easels, the *Immaculate Virgin* ascendant by Murillo; a full-scale *Deposition*, in that amalgam of distress and voluptuous luxury that few have understood as well as Van Dyck.

For the paintings of northern Europe—for English, Flemish and Dutch—you mount to the second and uppermost floor, past specimens of early English needlework, a vast decorative canvas by A. Bellucci (one of the early eighteenth-century Venetians imported by English patrons to embellish their new houses) of *The Family of Darius at the feet of Alexander the Great*, and a long case full of European porcelain. The English collection includes the sea-painter Brooking; Hogarth; Reynolds; Wilson;

OPPOSITE: Sir Joshua Reynolds: *Miss Keppel (Mrs. Thomas Meyrick)*. Canvas, *c.* 1782.

71

OPPOSITE: Sir Anthonie Van Dyck: *St. Augustine in Ecstasy*. Grisaille study for an altarpiece, 1628.

LEFT: Attributed to Sir Peter Paul Rubens: *Landscape: A Storm*. Canvas, *c.* 1628/29(?).

BELOW: Philips Koninck: *A View over Flat Country*. Canvas, *c.* 1655–60.

and especially the early Blake followers, Palmer, Calvert, Richmond; landscapes by Constable; a gap for Gainsborough in the main display has only recently been made good by the benefaction of the enchanting unfinished study of one of his daughters with a sheaf of corn, harvesting. Beyond that, Flemish and Dutch: a beautiful silvery suite of studies of landscape and others by Rubens and by Van Dyck; then Van Goyen, Ruysdael, Terbrugghen, Maes; a great stretch of Dutch lowlands under a vast Dutch sky by Philips Koninck. The Museum's collection of glass, mainly English drinking glasses, is also on the top floor, as is the astonishing Daisy Linda Ward bequest of Dutch still-life paintings, a collection of unique specialist importance, and an engaging counterpart to the Broughton collection of flower paintings in the sister institution, the Fitzwilliam at Cambridge.

There is one last appendix, though it is ignoble to refer to it as such, for it is famous amongst collectors and students of ceramics: the Marshall collection of Worcester porcelain and related pieces. This is rather difficult to find on the ground floor, through and beyond the spot-lit tomb culture of Egypt. The collection, displayed virtually complete, offers the most thorough representation that exists of the manufacture of the Worcester factory in its early period.

OPPOSITE: Abraham van Beyeren: *Still Life with a Silver Wine Jar and a Reflected Portrait of the Artist*. Canvas.

CHAPTER FIVE

THE ASHMOLEAN MUSEUM

HEBERDEN COIN ROOM
DEPARTMENT OF EASTERN ART
CAST GALLERY

C HARLES BULLER HEBERDEN WAS a classical scholar and a Principal of Brasenose College. In his will he left the university a thousand pounds, and in 1922, a year after his death, the Heberden Coin Room was opened. Heberden's bequest proved the catalyst that was to settle (though not immediately) the scattered and often confused history of the coin collections in the university and its colleges.

Early collectors of coins and medals tended not to see the two as distinct categories, but to use the term "medals" to embrace both; collectors of both were not, however, lacking in either numbers or enthusiasm. It was in the seventeenth century that a private "cabinet of medals" became a highly desirable constituent of a private library, if not an obligatory one. John Evelyn's *Numismata, or, A Discourse of Medals*, appeared in 1697 and thereafter a copy of it was to be found in most libraries of any pretension.

The earliest cabinets reflected the post-Renaissance fascination in classical antiquities, and almost all consisted of Greek and Roman specimens. Only a very few collectors could hope to rival the ambitious attempts of Charles I or the Earl of Arundel to import stone sculptures or inscriptions: for the rest, a collection of classical coins could be also a portable yet comprehensive collection of antiquities. The coins offered the substance of history: one could delicately pick up from the cabinet drawer the actual profile of, say, Augustus, or Nero, and hold it in the palm of the hand. Often one would be able to date the coin quite precisely (even though late numismatists have over and over again discovered that dating coins is not always as simple as it may seem). The prestige of the coins might be reflected in the splendour of the cabinets of drawers made to contain them—one example in the Coin Room is the most elegant cabinet that belonged to Charles Wentworth, 2nd Marquess of Rockingham, while a Louis XIV cabinet by Boulle (one of set of which others are still at Versailles) usually graces the Tapestry Gallery as a sumptuous piece in its own right.

The original University collections built gradually on the early gifts made through the agency of Laud, such as those of Barcham (1636) and Roe (1644), and were housed in the Bodleian. Tradescant owned medals, and numerous pages of the 1656 catalogue list them summarily. Ashmole added his, which were probably quite extensive (in spite of losses in a fire) and with a much stronger emphasis on coins. Numismatics were Ashmole's speciality: it was he who, according to Evelyn, "put in Order and Methodiz'd" the Royal Collection after the Restoration.

The collections remained apart until about 1860, when the Ashmolean coins along with the Ashmolean books side-stepped along Broad Street into the Bodleian. By 1885, Arthur Evans was already claiming that the "juxtaposition of the numismatic collections with our other antiquities is of vital importance for the sound study of Archaeology in the University", but their final establishment in the Ashmolean did not happen for about 35 years (1921). By then New College had already deposited its own collections in the Ashmolean, and after 1921 most other colleges followed suit—Balliol, Oriel, University, Corpus, Jesus, Keble, Magdalen and lastly (1940) came the great Christ Church collection.

In 1961 the stature and reputation of the Heberden Coin Room, now second in Britain only to that of the British Museum, were acknowledged by its establishment as a distinct department of the Museum, with its own Keeper (until then it had been part of the Department of Antiquities). By then, the quality and quantity of the three original components—the Bodleian, Ashmolean, and College collections—had been vastly expanded by a further formidable series of benefactions and some judicious buying. Sir Arthur Evans had given copiously in his lifetime; his bequest (1941) added yet more—for example, 6,000 Roman coins—and his memory was further saluted in 1944 by the purchase in his memory of the celebrated Crondall hoard of Anglo-Saxon and Merovingian or Continental gold coins— the prime surviving witness of the existence of a systematic Anglo-Saxon gold coinage in the seventh century A.D. Other benefactions have been scarcely less generous, and the collections also include Persian gold (the Eckstein collection, 1948); Indian (the T. B. Horwood collection, 1934); and Chinese (the R. Laird collection, 1947 and the von Halle collection, 1976); while since the war the prevailing patron was Sir Edward Robinson (d. 1976) under whose highly expert generosity the Greek collection, once patchy, has flowered into a major source for any student of the subject.

Numerically, the collection must now be approaching a quarter of a million items. It might seem to offer solid foundation for those often-heard complaints that museums keep most of their treasures hidden away "in the basement", for at most times there are not much more than 500 coins and medals on public display. But the collection, coins especially if not so much medals, is essentially an archive; and as befits a University collection, it is formed specifically for study and research. One or two of the Keeper staff normally hold joint appointments from the Visitors of the Ashmolean Museum and the Faculty of Literae Humaniores. Besides, the notion of being compelled to look at 250,000 coins on public display is a near nightmare. But apart from their historical importance, whether as individual items or as sequences, coins can have their own beauty, and a beauty of considerable variety, ranging from the chunky silver of Greece, with the bold if often mysterious allusions of their imprinted designs, through the formidable portraiture of much Roman; the high and finished sophistication of the great European mints of the Renaissance and after, or the heavy holed copper of the Chinese. There are fine sculptural achievements to be found in the miniature compass of coins, and sometimes in unexpected places—I always feel that the finest English coinage was that of Oliver Cromwell—but the famous masterpieces are medallic. A selection of the great medals of the Italian Renaissance, from Pisanello on, are shown in the galleries of Western Art, in context with the applied arts of the period.

Department of Eastern Art
Eastern Art is the youngest of the Ashmolean departments. Founded in 1962 by the merger of the collections once in the former Indian Institute and those (mainly Chinese) in the former Department of Fine Art, it has consolidated and increased in all its component subjects. In most of them the Museum now ranks after only the British Museum and the Victoria and Albert Museum in importance in Britain.

The perfect and immaculate silence of the early ceramics, from the Han through to the Sung Dynasties, are admirably represented, especially the fine range of Yüeh wares. The examples of celadon—that misleading term for anything of that lovely grey-green colour—are superb. Their long popularity in Europe is attested to by a celadon bowl with European silver-gilt mounts at New College which belonged to Archbishop Warham at the beginning of the sixteenth century. The Lung-ch'uan type (a fine example is in the collection, from the Ingram gift) of the Sung period, with a thick, slightly misty, slightly bluish glaze, and usually wonderfully simple in form, was especially popular.

Through the cases we can see the transition from stoneware to true porcelain. Some ware of the T'ang Dynasty A.D. (618–906 is already virtually true porcelain; and the beautiful clear

shallow dishes with incised relief, as if hovering in the depths of the clear glaze, of Ting ware from the Sung Dynasty (A.D. 980–1278) have never been surpassed. There is always a remarkable variety of forms, and ceramic figures or models are of course great favourites, ranging from the tomb model of a cooking stove (Han Dynasty: 206 B.C.–A.D. 220) to the well-known T'ang horses and camels and the delightful little model of an outdoor earth-closet, delicate as a rococo *tempietto* in a chinoiserie garden.

From the very early periods, all forms of bronzes are well represented. These range from the solid, homely, cooking-pot type pieces with bold decoration, to the strange, stiff-legged tripod drinking cups and the circular bronze mirrors. Here, as with celadon, it is the colour, the patina that long burial has bloomed upon the bronze, that is a great part of the attraction for modern European eyes; it is perhaps discourteous to reflect that the makers of these bronzes probably assigned them to the tombs bright and beastly as brass, and liked them so.

Chinese blue-and-white, the popularity of which has never entirely vanished since Rossetti and Whistler went over-

T'ang Dynasty, China, A.D. 618–905: Earthenware tomb model of a bullock cart.

OPPOSITE: Greek coins (enlarged) from the Heberden Coin Room.
a) Tetradachm showing owl. Athens, *c*. 430 B.C.
b) Tetradrachm showing Alexander the Great (336–323 B.C.).
c) Decadrachm showing racing quadriga. Syracuse, *c*. 395 B.C.

79

Shang Dynasty, China, tenth to eleventh century B.C.: Bronze "kuei".

board for it from the 1860s onwards, comes in with the Ming Dynasty (A.D. 1368–1644). There are also fine examples of the rare (because rarely successful and never entirely mastered) technique of under-glaze painting in red. The blue doubtless came from the influence of the Middle East—contacts with China are sometimes said to go back to the first century B.C. One type of later Chinese porcelain, much loved in the West for obvious reasons, is also especially well represented—armorial porcelain, plates and other pieces made for the eighteenth-century European taste in *chinoiserie*—whole services ordered from Europe with the family arms of the client. There are also some excellent *blanc-de-chine* figures. *Blanc-de-chine* is a medium that, when of low quality, can be quite extraordinarily vapid. When good, however, it achieves a tension between the vigour and rhythm of its handling and form, and the abstract transparency of its material, that can be mesmerising. Lacquer—an acquired taste for many, owing again to the prevalence of indifferent examples in Europe, but likewise fascinating when of high quality—is also well represented; so too are Korean wares, with often a less sophisticated feeling than the Chinese, but delightfully spontaneous. Sculpture in bronze,

Ming Dynasty, China, fourteenth century
A.D. Porcelain, blue and white stem bowl.

stone and wood are included, and Chinese painting too is represented—the collection of modern Chinese painting being perhaps
the best in the country.

The Japanese collection is less extensive but when Gerald
Reitlinger's great gift, already deeded to Oxford, finally comes to
the Ashmolean the collection as a whole—for ceramics—will be
perhaps the most complete in Britain. The collection of *tsuba* (over
a thousand pieces in the study collection) is outstanding, and those
of *ojime*, *inro* and *netsuke* very fine. There is also an admirable
general representation of the development of Japanese ceramics—
Satsuma wares especially, and tea-ceremony wares. Japanese
paintings, prints—from the eighteenth century to contemporary
artists—are represented.

Westward there is representation of the arts of Burma,
Siam, Cambodia, Java and even Tibet. India is as well shown as
anywhere in Britain outside the British and the Victoria and
Albert Museums. The British failed, however, in the period of the
British *raj*, to take advantage of the artistic loot available (for
which India is now grateful). Moghul miniature paintings the
imperialists did collect, but most of the world of Hindu art fell on
blind British eyes. An exception to this rule is the Gandhara

sculpture from the northwest, where the European classical influence borne in by Alexander's armies had such decisive and enduring influence. Still, the more purely Indian styles, in stone, terracotta and bronze, are engagingly represented, and there are some masterpieces of high order—the "Oxford" terracotta plaque; the Siva head from Mathura; a superb Buddha from Bodhgaya.

Nor is Islamic art neglected. Metalware, rare early glass, but above all ceramics: the brilliant wares from Persia and Arabia, the enchanting decoration of the Isnik potters from Turkey. These mostly come from the formidable collection of Sir Alan Barlow and, as elsewhere in the Museum, Eastern Art's debt to a series of remarkable collectors is enormous: to the Ingrams, Sayces, Malletts and Farrers, the Murray-Aynsleys and the Hoernles of past generations; to present collectors and benefactors like Eric North and Gerald Reitlinger. These are all collectors of great discrimination and learning, and their help to the Museum lies not only in the gift of splendid masterpieces, but also in the creation of great study collections to benefit future generations of students.

The Cast Gallery
Now that the cult of the "original" can become only too easily a fetish, the value of collections of casts tends to be ignored, or at best underestimated. This is a waste, for even in these days of instant jet-travel and ubiquitous broadcasting of images via photography, the three-dimensional reproduction can still contain or reflect the potency of the original to a very high degree of faithfulness.

The rather hidden entrance to the Cast Gallery is off the passage connecting St. John Street to St. Giles Street across the bleak northern backside of the Ashmolean Museum proper. It does not perhaps offer immediate access to Greece—the charioteer from Delphi undeniably looks different here from how he would in a Mediterranean light. On the other hand, you do get the shock that compressed juxtaposition and dizzy differences of scales of so many of the most famous images in the world, all cheek by jowl, can produce.

The Cast Gallery is in fact a magic experience. The upper floor, at which level you enter, is a bit disconcerting but does not batter at the senses. On a brown polished parquet floor, on brown painted plinths, the casts are ordered in their regiment. They reproduce works of down to about the middle of the fifth century B.C. and of later copies after these: bruised heads from the west pediment of the Temple of Zeus at Olympia; works by Myron of Eleutherae. Here are famous images like the Discobolus, an example of the compromise that casts can consolidate: the body comes from a version in the Vatican, the head from another one in the Termae. Here stand the archaic Greek images with slant

OPPOSITE: Kitagawa Utamaro: *Girl Holding a Tea-bowl.* Woodblock colour print.

83

eyes, frizzled hair as if by permanent wave, and those disquieting almost smirking curves of lips; and supreme amongst them that matchless charioteer from Delphi.

To descend thence to the lower level of the Gallery is like being dropped without transition into one of the more tormented circles of Dante's Inferno. This is because you come down the stairs steeply into the field of force exerted by the Parthenon frieze, which here, confined in small piece, appears both gigantic and possessed by demonic energy. Farther on, all is calmer, though still strange: why go to Paris or Rome, when you can see here Venus de Milo and the Winged Victory of Samothrace from the Louvre, standing within arm's length from each other and from the Vatican's Apollo Belvedere. Here is the Laocoon, the Belvedere Torso, that elegiac boy with a thorn in his foot. Here the great Mausoleus from the British Museum takes on the air of a colossal sketch by Rodin for Balzac, and Demosthenes (whose fine head in stone you can see amongst Antiquities in the Ashmolean galleries) is provided with a body.

Such galleries of casts are rooted in the nineteenth-century emphasis on a classical education, on art as defined within classical and then Renaissance terms of reference. The one at Oxford began as a ready to hand auxiliary to the teaching of form and style—and it still serves as such, while the Lincoln Professor of Classical Archaeology is still the Gallery's honorary Curator, and so (in part) a member of the Ashmolean staff. There are only two comparable collections in Britain: the rather larger one at Cambridge, and that at University College, London (the enormous collection at the Victoria and Albert Museum is mainly concerned with post-classical work). The quality of the best of the casts—that is, their quality as faithful reproductions irrespective of the quality of the originals—will surprise an eye accustomed to thinking of casts as those bland busts of Bach or Beethoven mass-produced for music-shops. True, they are almost all plaster, but the fidelity to the texture even of marble or bronze can be remarkable. Though the Charioteer's eyelashes may be bleared, as the label remarks, the total impact of that superb bronzed image, of concentrated stillness in its austere height, is marvellous. Especially perhaps if you penetrate to it from a bleakly drizzling Oxford winter forenoon.

CHAPTER SIX

OTHER UNIVERSITY INSTITUTIONS

Bodley is a name to conjure with, the learned world over. The Bodleian Library may not be as big as the British Museum Library (say a mere three million compared with six million books), but it is more glamorous and also more humane and, I swear it, more welcoming. If in a hurry, you may miss it: the entrance is on the wonderfully withdrawn Schools Quadrangle, severe yet commodious with the names of the old Schools—Geometry, Arithmetic, etc.—blazoned in blue and gold over its doorways. The carved heads over the doorways are mostly of early this century (by E. A. Hammond) and represent mainly long-gone heroes of learning and letters. Much more recent, by the archway leading to Radcliffe Square, are Edmund Craster (Bodley's Librarian 1931–45), and Dean Lowe of Christ Church; and, by the passage to the Clarendon Building, J. N. L. Myres, who was Bodley's Librarian till 1966, and a Registrar, Sir Douglas Veale. All these are by Mark Batten. On the courtyard site of the main gateway an intransigently splendid statement of Jacobean importance, rising through five tiers with a vast panel showing James I in full relief attended by Fame and the kneeling University. On the other side (west) of the quad is a stately pompous bronze statue of the Earl of Pembroke, one-time Chancellor, and benefactor, of the university. This was made in the 1630s by Le Sueur. It was originally at Wilton (the family house) but a later Earl of Pembroke gave it to the university in 1722 (the university envoys are said to have removed the head and borne it back with them to Oxford, to make sure the body would follow). Behind him is the entrance to the Library via the Proscholium.

The prime function of the Library is not to exhibit but to make books and manuscripts available to individual readers as

Hubert le Sueur: *William Herbert, 3rd Earl of Pembroke*. Bronze, *c.* 1640(?).

OPPOSITE: French illuminated manuscript: *The Romance of Alexander*. Mid-fourteenth century.

and when they are wanted. Accordingly there are only temporary exhibitions on specific themes, or simply a more-or-less arbitrary choice of the Bodleian treasures. These are formidable in their artistic range and in their wealth, especially of course in both Eastern and Western illuminated manuscripts. For the study of the illuminated book, the Bodleian is one of the great store-houses in the world. For the study of British painting of up to 1500, illuminations are the main source of material: mediaeval mural painting has vanished far more completely than they, owing both to the religious iconoclasms of the sixteenth and seventeenth centuries, and to the dampness of the climate that causes walls to shed applied colour as if afflicted by incurable dermatitis. From almost the beginning of Bodley's foundation, the manuscripts have poured in, many just salvaged from the dispersal of the great libraries of the monasteries at the Reformation. And later benefactions have never quite ceased. Though medals and other objects from the great Douce bequest went to the Ashmolean, his manuscripts stayed in Bodley, which had already received Ashmole's manuscripts from the Old Ashmolean. More recently, several of the College libraries richest in manuscripts have deposited them on permanent loan to the Bodleian.

The English illuminations range from the Romanesque up to the van Eyckian naturalism of the fifteenth and sixteenth centuries: from spectacular early examples, like the superbly formalised Ms. Ashmole 511, a *Bestiary* with its famous whale and its magical Christ Creator of the Stars, through the great Douce *Apocalypse*, one of the finest of thirteenth-century manuscripts, to the later Books of Hours. The continental schools are also represented in some depth, even to exotic rarities like the Kennicott Bible from Corunna in Spain (the most lavishly decorated of all Hebrew manuscripts), and a magnificent series of middle and late Byzantine illuminations of the tenth to fifteenth centuries. There is also Islamic graphic art, especially those brilliantly lucid illuminations of the Persian schools and of the Indian Mughal style which are now so coveted by collectors the world over. (The first of them to come to the University was presented by Archbishop Laud in 1639.)

The Bodleian also houses other works of art, like the sigh-provoking sequence of drawings by J. C. Buckler (1811–27) of Oxford as she was—her picturesque prime before despoliation by traffic, road signs, tourists, hygiene and street lighting. Also present are associative objects for sentiment: a clutch of objects relating to P. B. Shelley including some (alleged) portraits; a chair carved out of the timbers of Drake's *Golden Hind*.

The Proscholium is the Library's shop counter, where are displayed its publications and the dazzling sample of its wares set out in postcard form. Its walls contain a handsome sampling of Bodley's large collection of painted portraits. Here you may find paintings of local heroes—of Bodley, Laud, Camden, Clarendon,

St. Dunstan at the feet of Christ. A drawing, probably from Glastonbury, of the mid-tenth century. The fourteenth-century inscription attributes the drawing to St. Dunstan himself.

OPPOSITE: Cornelius Ketel: *Sir Martin Frobisher*. Oil on canvas, 1577.

and Lord Crew, Bishop of Durham (a formal rendering, but also one of Sir Godfrey Kneller's most successful pieces of painting). Curiously, in the midst of these fairly staid effigies, there is also a bustling whole-length of the pistol-carrying Elizabethan venturer and explorer, Sir Martin Frobisher, signed and dated by the Dutch painter Cornelius Ketel, 1577. This was given to the University in 1674 by Dr Charleton; by then the Bodleian, as we have already noted, provided the University and Oxford with their main picture gallery. The portraits of academic and local worthies are dispersed through the various reading rooms and elsewhere in the Bodleian—the Curators' Room, for example, has an impressive sequence of the successive librarians—but application to see any specific one must be made in advance. They are catalogued by Mrs. Poole in the first volume of her great *Catalogue of Oxford Portraits*, and she lists well over 300 portraits in the Bodleian.

Since she wrote, some have been dispersed—a few of the finest have gone to the Ashmolean, such as Pierce's magnificent bust of the young Christopher Wren. However, there are still a remarkable number left in the Bodleian.

Off the stairs that rise from the Proscholium are, near the bottom, another small exhibition area used for temporary displays, and then, at the top of that long and ancient ascent of shallow steps, Arts End, the only part of the Library proper that the passing visitor may view. Before entering it you can sight, through the glass door of the Upper Reading Room, the painted frieze of over 200 heads of famous men of letters, scholars and divines. Painted about 1618–20, it later vanished from sight for some centuries, and was recovered and restored (by Clive Rouse) in the 1960s; the quality is coarse but assertive. The portraits, many of course imaginary, go from Aristotle on—Aquinas, Wycliff, Huss, Luther, closing in the dour physiognomies of Elizabethan divines. Arts End is lined with books (claimed as the earliest surviving wall-shelving) and a lowish richly decorated wood ceiling, repeating innumerable blazoned coats-of-arms. At the entry to Duke Humphrey's Library, two busts face each other high on the walls. Bodley himself is here, "carved to the life by an excellent hand at London" and given by the Chancellor (the Earl of Dorset) in 1605—that is, in Bodley's lifetime. He is in stone (rather livelier than in his monument in Merton Chapel), and confronts Charles I in bronze, by Le Sueur, given by Laud in 1636 (subsequently banished, but replaced in 1661 after payment for "polishing ye rust from ye King's Picture"). Down the walls, you can see the painted portraits hanging as, no doubt, they always used to hang all through the Library.

The architectural quality of the repositories in which Oxford stores its collection is admirable, and admirably various. The *University Museum*, linked with the Pitt Rivers Museum, is a masterpiece in its way although the collections which it was made to house were not considered art. The interior of the Museum is breathtaking: a single large space with a gallery around, and soaring steeply in glass and iron. The wrought-iron decoration (made by the Coventry firm of Skidmore) of the columns is brilliant in execution and paradoxically light in its fantasy, sometimes anticipating *art nouveau* but much less self-conscious. The stone carving, on piers and columns of the ambulatory and gallery, is equally crisp and inventive; it includes work of the unruly O'Shea family from Dublin, and Ruskin himself is said to have joined in—this applies mainly to the west side, the carving elsewhere is later. Around the sides there are whole-length statues of heroes of science, from Aristotle, Roger Bacon, Harvey to Darwin (lackadaisical, leaning slightly back with one leg crossed over the other). They are by various sculptors—Armstead, Weekes, Durham, H. R. Pinker (his is the Darwin) and others—but the most attractive sculpture is the relief head of the Museum's architect, Benjamin Woodward, by Alexander Munro (the most consistent of sculptors associated with the Pre-Raphaelites). Woodward died in 1861, soon after the Museum was finished.

The sealed-in conservation and lighting of the exhibits in the Museum, which stems from a resolution of 1849 to assemble "all the materials explanatory of the organic beings placed upon the globe", makes it difficult for them to consort happily with the lofty aerial space of the building. The sentimental visitor should note, even if blinkering himself to scientific instruction, one case in particular: it contains the remnants of what is perhaps the most famous of the exhibits in the original museums of the Tradescants and of Ashmole—the Dodo.

The *Pitt Rivers Museum* was built on to the University Museum in 1885–6. It has developed from the collections by Lieutenant-General Henry Lane-Fox Pitt Rivers (1827–1900) who gave in 1883 some 15,000 specimens. There are now over a million, and for a happy moment on entering, the visitor could be forgiven for thinking every one of them was on permanent display. Amongst them is some former Ashmolean material, transferred from the Ashmolean in 1886. Like Christ Church's great benefactor, General Guise, Pitt Rivers was one of those excellent military men far from confined to the study of tactics, latrines and other soldierly affairs, but gifted with an alert inquiring mind liable to be kindled by alien and exotic subjects. Once kindled, the mind would move at a spanking pace to the full exploration of these subjects. In Pitt Rivers' case, the stimulus to exploration seems to have come from close scrutiny of the development of the common smooth-bore percussion musket (known as "Brown Bess" to the troops) into the rifle. Discerning in this development an evolutionary process, he started collections to illustrate stages of such progressions and the often minute changes of detail that gradually modified them. His collection included weapons, of course, from flint arrowheads onwards, and also all kinds of implements. By 1900, when he died, the stature to which he had grown was indicated in an obituary notice where he is described as "without any exaggeration, one of the first men of this century as an anthropologist and exact antiquary".

Pitt Rivers' range as a collector was almost unlimited, for all human artefacts were relevant to his theme. Yet he was systematic; "his precept", wrote the historian of the Museum, Beatrice Blackwood, "that Ethnology and Archaeology are the present and past of the same subject . . . has always been a guiding principle in the functioning of the Pitt Rivers Museum." He grouped objects according to a series of main groups "in which objects of like form or formation from all over the world were associated to form series, each of which illustrated as completely as possible the varieties under which a given art, industry or appliance occurred" (Henry Balfour). Within these groups, local sub-groups could be identified.

Two Nigerian bronzes from Benin.

Like Sir Arthur Evans, he was formidable in his energy and endowed with the private means to deploy it to maximum effect. A scientific and scrupulous archaeologist, he excavated in several parts of the world. In local excavations, he is said to have been wont to arrive on the site in his carriage followed by his team, wearing his colours, on a shoal of pennyfarthing bicycles. The finds of these excavations, much of them on or near his inherited estate, Cranborne Chase, together with other series, remained in family possession at Farnham in north Dorset; after various tribulations the residue of these is being established in a museum in Salisbury. His other collections he gave to Oxford in 1883, and they are still housed mainly in the building constructed for them, linked to the east flank of the University Museum.

The present setting lacks the architectural quality of its immediate neighbour the Museum. It is a simple Court, with

galleries and a glassed roof, but the immediate impression it gives is powerful: silent squads of serried showcases packed tight, dominated by the column, forty-foot high, of the totem pole from Queen Charlotte Islands, British Columbia, that rises through the well of the court. The specimens are packed tight, not just in showcases but under them too and (in the galleries) in the ceiling. In 1874 the General denied he collected with any purpose of surprising anyone, either by the rarity or value of the objects exhibited, but solely with a view to instruction. For this purpose, ordinary and typical specimens, just as much as rare objects, have been selected for permanent exhibition. These are arranged in sequence so as to trace the succession of ideas by which the minds of men in a primitive condition of culture have progressed from the simple to the complex, and from the homogeneous to the heterogeneous.

The General may deny surprise, but few will fail to be surprised. And surprised not only on the first visit, but on each subsequent one. Only yesterday it seems, the Pitt Rivers display would have been sniffed out of court as drearily old-fashioned; old-fashioned it is, but now meritoriously so. Object lies cheek by jowl with object, with minute often hand-written labels attendant: over them prowl the raiding eyes of child, adolescent and adult, accompanied by clucks, coos and murmurations. Pure pleasure is the greatest offering the Pitt Rivers has for the general public, though all the while it is a serious instrument of teaching for the student. Shrunken heads of enemies of the Jivaro Indians; a brilliant geometric cloak of feathers from Hawaii; a ceremonial mask from New Guinea, topped by a dappled fish a metre and a half tall)—these are objects which few are likely to have seen before. Pull back a curtain and there are musical instruments from all the cultures of the world. Pitt Rivers and his successors over the last 100 years started just in time, before culture became a self-conscious word that tends to preen itself as if in front of a mirror. The processes that these artefacts chart are being killed stone-dead, year after quick year, in the progress of industrialisation, mass-production and nostalgic faking for tourist purposes. Yet a plastered skull with cowrie shells for eyes, from New Guinea perhaps and of our own century, may be all but identical with the skull of 8,000 years ago from Jericho that you can see in the Ashmolean Museum.

Most of the collection has been gathered over the last century, but some objects are earlier. Some of the Tradescants' pieces that are now called ethnographical are still enthroned in the Ashmolean, though others were transferred to the Pitt Rivers, as was also the splendid loot of Captain Cook's second voyage to the Pacific Islands (acquired direct by the Ashmolean from Reinhold Forster, official "curator" on the voyage, after his return in 1775).

The latest foundation amongst the University museums, the *Museum of the History of Science* on Broad Street (1925), is also paradoxically the oldest of the University museums. It inhabits the original building of the Ashmolean—built, probably by the very gifted local master-mason Thomas Wood, in 1678–83—from which the original Tradescant/Ashmolean collections were dispersed to the present Ashmolean and elsewhere, from 1886 on.

The beginnings of the History of Science Museum are vested in a family to whom Oxford owes an incalculable debt, the Evanses. Lewis Evans (brother of Sir Arthur) "could not spell, but liked blowing himself up with chemicals", notes their half-sister Dame Joan Evans. Five years before his death in 1930 he had given his very remarkable collection of early scientific instruments to Oxford, and his gift formed the nucleus of the Museum. To begin with the Museum occupied only the upper floor, but in 1940 the whole building was made over to it. Since then the collection has been enlarged by other benefactors, so that now it is

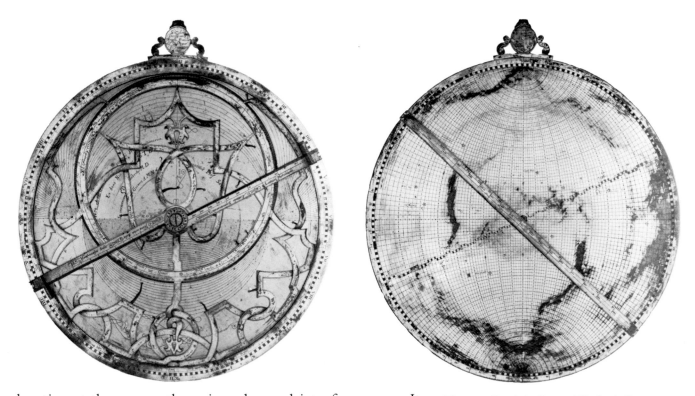

bursting at the seams—the universal complaint of museums. It remains, however, a site for calm reflection on the mutability of human affairs. Slightly withdrawn from the normally busy Broad, it holds a silence articulated by the generous rises of its staircase where occasionally footsteps sound, and by the passing of time. A few timepieces tick or chime, but scores of others rest, as if the vanity of recording and measuring time had at last been recognised.

Thomas Gemini: Queen Elizabeth I's astrolabe, 1559.

The history of the measurement of time, of the observation of the heavens, is a prime concern of this museum, expressed in materials of singular complex elegance—sundials, calendars and almanacs, armillary spheres, astrolabes—many of them outstanding examples of the metalworker's art. Astrolabes were the subject of a treatise by Chaucer (of which the Bodleian has an illuminated fifteenth-century manuscript); they were highly functional, for the measuring of altitudes, but like armillary spheres seem also to have challenged their makers' sense of design. The collection here is unrivalled. That of microscopes is claimed as "almost complete" in its historical sense; they too own a fascination for the eye, though safe in their cases, for they necessarily cannot be used by the casual visitor. Mostly they stand like miniature batteries of anti-aircraft guns trained downwards rather than up, with ordered reserves of alternative lenses like shell-cases. And there is one splendid, dotty example of the niceties of the fine arts being applied: the silver universal microscope made by George Adams for George III—as though an *épergne* had had an illicit affair with a candelabrum, producing as by-blow a unique piece of table ware

Thomas Tompion and George Graham:
Orrery. Silver and ebony, *c.* 1710.

for some intellectual feast, all adorned with draped classical male and female figures, *putti*, urns. Microscopes are matched by a sequence of telescopes, and some apparatus once in the Radcliffe Observatory.

Upstairs the premises are labeled as of the original *Musaeum Ashmoleanum*; downstairs is the *Officia Chimica*, once the University chemical laboratory. Clocks are mainly down-stairs, though they also accompany the visitors up and down the stairs themselves, some happily still vocal, and include a fine representation of Oxford regional clock-makers. Clocks and watches derive mainly from the Beeson, Barnett and Iliffe collections, and, with the collections in the Ashmolean, constitute a formidable hoard for study by any horologist. The Ashmolean emphasis (the Mallet and Bullivant collections) is mainly on the artistry of the cases, but the Museum of the History of Science has many elegant and interesting ones too, and in the Beeson Room there is a mesmeric scatter of them in a low circular case over a mirror, like a clear pool with goldfish. Elsewhere downstairs there are many things. Amongst early chemical apparatus are retorts—in glass, porcelain, fireclay, glazed earthenware—of strange yet elemental-seeming shapes, and dead apparatus can often assume an enduring significance almost distinct from its status as historic evidence. Watkins and Hills' Electrostatic Generator of around 1850 may well raise echoes of memories of some twentieth-century abstract sculpture. Elsewhere, art in its illustrative or recording capacity spills vividly across the history of science. Einstein's blackboard, with its magic formula still chalked on it as he left it at an Oxford lecture in May, 1931, becomes for most pure totem or relic. Of peculiar interest is the Gunther Collection of Japanese *netsuke* of subjects relating to medicine: for example, a miniature of a man admiring his enormous cyst in a mirror. There are also elements surviving of the original Ashmolean bequest—zoological specimens, horns, antlers, swordfishes' swords—perhaps the oldest surviving specimens of their kind, and some going back to the Tradescants. There is Dr. Jenner's chair, early surgical instruments, and one or two other museums virtually complete in this museum: notably, in a stout and impressive oak box, the *Musaeum Pointerianum* from a bequest from John Poynter to St John's (which lends it here) about 1720—"several sorts of Rarities", including what may be the earliest surviving collection of birds' eggs.

Oxford is fairly rich in public statuary. Throughout the central area, the perambulator can collect gesturing frozen figures, gargoyles, bosses; mostly they are applied to or even part of actual architecture, so it seems relevant to point to some within their setting. I take therefore two routes, one to the right, or east and south, as you come out of the Old Ashmolean building, and the other to the left, or west and north. Of course I can offer no more than a token sampling of the vivid detailing that can be found all through the centre. Among the most vivid or attractive examples is the sequence of gigantic Emperors' heads that Christopher Wren wrapped about the curved front of his Sheldonian Theatre. Through the centuries they have compelled fascination, loathing, affection and myth (see *Zuleika Dobson*), though they are not what they were. The originals, presumably of 1669 when the Sheldonian was finished, were worn out by 1868, and replaced by new ones, replaced in their turn by new ones between 1968–76 (by Michael Black). The originals, in a state of blurred and attractive decay, are dotted about Oxford (two, for example, in Worcester gardens); others are said to have moved as far as Herefordshire. In the Sheldonian itself, the painted ceiling by Robert Streeter features the Triumph of Religion, Arts and Science over Envy, Hatred and Malice, contrived as if strung on ropes like the velarium of a Roman theatre. It is a *trompe-l'oeil* convention, but Streeter's skill, and his command of seventeenth-century artistic convention in general, were neither good enough nor free enough to *tromper* a twentieth-century eye: the result is curious, very large, and unconvincing. Reverting to statuary, one may seek two statues, of Archbishop Sheldon and of the Duke of Ormonde, both by Sir Henry Cheere, 1737, but perhaps in vain (they are said by Nikolaus Pevsner to be in the basement).

Next door at the Clarendon Building, now annexed by the Bodleian, Clarendon himself, Lord Chancellor, historian and Chancellor of the University (by Francis Bird, 1721) is in a niche on the west side. But most eloquent is the sky-line, accented by the gestures of the Muses all but two of which were designed in lead by Thornhill. (The exceptions were added in 1975 by the Blackwell family: they have to watch them from their bookselling premises across the road and perhaps the gap of the missing Muses became oversensitive, like missing teeth.) In the Clarendon Building, the gorgeous iron grille is by that great master Tijou, while inside, in a room once assigned to the delegates of the Press, are retrospective busts of Laud and Clarendon, again by Cheere.

South through the Schools quadrangle, whereabouts fine sculpture is not lacking (see p. 85), and past the Radcliffe Camera: Radcliffe himself is in a niche over the entrance, by Rysbrack, 1744–7. And amongst busts within, there are two fine ones by Rysbrack also: the architect, James Gibbs, 1726; and a terracotta, very free, identified as one Francis Smith, 1741. Across Radcliffe Square to the University Church, St. Mary's: on the High Street side, the statue of the Virgin over the porch with twisted column by Nicholas Stone (1637) is bruised but touchingly tender still. (It was cited against Archbishop Laud in his trial as evidence of his doctrinal luxuriousness.) St. Mary's furnishings are oddly bleak, though there are some good memorial tablets. The statues once on the tower are to be found in New College and All Souls (see pp. 113 and 122). Bearing (a long way) east down the High, opposite Magdalen, the gateways of the Botanic Gardens are again by Nicholas Stone (1632/3); the main gateway is profusely ornate, sculpture perhaps rather than architecture, but the statues in it are later.

Reverting back now to the starting point, the Old Ashmolean building in Broad Street, if you proceed thence the other way, left and west, you can discover almost at once a most resonant piece of non-sculpture: a little cross-mark set flush in the middle of the Broad (just about opposite the Master of Balliol's front door). That was where Cranmer, Ridley and Latimer were burned alive in 1555 (the Broad was then the town ditch); contemplation of that inset mark may cause hiatus in the mind on the sunniest of Oxford afternoons. The actual Martyrs' Memorial is round the corner at the end of the Broad and at the start of St. Giles: a depressive object, designed by George Gilbert Scott, 1841–3, echoing the pattern of Eleanor Crosses, in a drear Gothic. The three martyrs (all carved by H. Weekes) look weary, which is probably realistic but not inspiring. The statues briskly confronting them from the Taylorian on the west side of St. Giles are both, almost unbelievably, contemporaneous with the images of the Gothic martyrs, and much more exhilarating even though they improbably represent France, Italy, Germany and Spain (all by W. G. Nicholl).

Considerably further north and west, in beside the buildings of the Radcliffe Infirmary, is that enchantingly idiosyncratic building, the Radcliffe Observatory. The Observatory was begun by Keene in 1772 and finished by Wyatt, 1794; like the Botanic Gardens gate, it appears more as a large eccentric sculpture than as architecture. In fact it is a tower, though with very pretty reliefs of the Winds (by Bacon, 1792–4); and, topping all, also by Bacon, the lead group of Hercules and Atlas supporting a copper globe.

Amongst University buildings one must mention the Union, off St. Michael's Street. For here ought to be other famous wall-paintings, fruit of that high spirited Pre-Raphaelite venture when Morris, Rossetti, Burne-Jones, Arthur Hughes and others all set about bringing art to the Union in 1857. Unfortunately they were not very well versed in mural techniques, and though Morris refreshed part of it in 1875, and Professor Tristram tried again thoroughly in 1930, the desired impression of brilliant mediaeval illumination is faded, inert, and almost evaporated.

CHAPTER SEVEN

THE COLLEGES

Christ Church and the Cathedral

CHRIST CHURCH SETS ITSELF apart from other colleges. It refuses to call itself a college and regards anyone else who does so with an expression ranging from indifference to a severe sniff. Referring to itself as *The House*, it refers back to its status as *Aedes Christi* rather than *Collegium Christi*, which all relates in turn to the fact that its "college" chapel is also the Cathedral. Once St. Frideswide's Priory, it fell in 1522 to Cardinal Wolsey who translated it into "Cardinal College". Wolsey fell in his turn to Henry VIII, who refounded it in 1532 under the name of King Henry VIII's College. Then in 1546 the King melded it with his new bishopric of Oxford, which he had first vested in Osney Abbey, as *Ecclesia Christi Cathedralis Oxoniensis*, which is, in brief, Christ Church. Echoes of Osney here persist: the entrance, Tom Tower, is voiced by Great Tom, which is cast from metal that once sounded in the long-vanished tower of Osney Abbey.

Christ Church should be entered from St. Aldate's Street through Tom Tower. The bottom of Tom Tower is Wolsey's, of the 1520s, the upper part Christopher Wren's (1681–2). In a niche central in Wren's window is a belated salute to the first founder, Wolsey, in the shape of a statue of him by the best English baroque sculptor, Francis Bird, 1719. The Cardinal here is indeed very baroque in ample, embracing gesture, but wind and rain have worn away his features. Inside, the statue facing east is Queen Anne, put up in 1706 (perhaps by the then popular sculptor John Nost), but inside is also that great and spacious quadrangle. Central to that, the pool called Mercury, after the statue poised in its centre. This is a copy of Giovanni da Bologna and not the first here. The first image of Mercury, by William Bird, was installed in 1670; a replacement (with bronze head and lead body) was savaged in 1817 by the future Lord Derby, Prime Minister; only in 1928 was the present (lead) version installed on a base specially designed by Sir Edwin Lutyens.

Wolsey appears again, full length, with cardinal's hat and staff; but here more comfortably and stoutly placid, and indeed blessing, between two female figures on Bodley's Tower, all of about 1876–8. Likewise blessing, in a canopied niche in the opposite angle, a former head of the House, Bishop John Fell (1625–86). He is sometimes described as the second (or third) Founder, and was, if in more restricted circumstances, as autocratic as Wolsey; the statue is dated 1877 and replaced an original, of about 1722, which was translated to the gardens at Nuneham Park.

The complex anatomy of the Cathedral, contained within those massive twelfth-century flanks that flower with such an irresistible combination of grace and awkwardness into the late fifteenth-century traceried vault, is analysed in detail by Nikolaus Pevsner. Its rich architecture is answered by a richness of furniture, and although its tombs and memorials may not match the grandest effigies of some cathedrals, it has a rare and very various wealth of monumental lapidary inscription on tablets and cartouches. Decorative memorials and furniture provide a wide variety: the striking early stiff-leaf carving on capitals (especially north transept) of the late twelfth century; the naturalistic foliage with a mad-merry face amongst it, on the fragments of St. Frideswide's shrine, perhaps 1289; and the base of a cross, probably earlier in the thirteenth century in the gallery over the vestry. There are also Burne-Jones windows (a very early and spectacular one, 1859, is in the Latin Chapel) and the furnishings of Scott's restorations, not least the elaborate reredos by G. F. Bodley. The earliest glass is the celebrated Thomas-à-Becket window with its piece of blank glass where the saint's head should be. The head was expunged, it is said, at Henry VIII's command; the glass, of *c.* 1340, is of splendid intensity. There is an especially excellent example of the van Linges, that glazier family so well represented in Oxford. In this case it is Abraham van Linge, dating from in the 1630s, of Jonah with a fairy-tale romantic vision of Nineveh ramping up a hill beyond (north aisle of nave). The nineteenth-century representation includes, besides the several Burne-Jones windows, a peculiarly crammed and striking example of Clayton and Bell's work, 1872 (north transept).

Of memorials to characters whose memory still lives in national history, two are the most interesting. The Stuart memorial, black-gowned bust in sculptured oval, of Robert Burton (d. 1639), author of the *Anatomy of Melancholy* (north transept); and in the nave that to the philosopher Bishop Berkeley (d. 1753), a plain but elegantly distinguished memorial with an epitaph from Alexander Pope. Also in the nave is a good profile of the don-architect Dean Aldrich by Sir Henry Cheere, 1732. There is a handsome crowd, of charming melancholy variety, in the south transept: a strange conversation piece of two courtiers, Lord and Lady Brouncker, small-scale whole-lengths kneeling at a table in contemplation of a skull, about 1650; Lord Mounslowe (1683), with a nice accumulation of attributes, urn, martial trophies, but also books in low relief on their shelves down one side; a very grand monument by a rare sculptor, J. Latham, *c.* 1670 to Viscount Grandison. In the south aisle of the nave, note a reverend don, Edward Pocock (1691), facing up to eternity in a mortarboard, a gallant gesture.

The Cathedral lost its plate in the Reformation, and the College lost its in the Civil Wars. The Cathedral however has notably a massive and elaborate Communion service of 1660–61, given by Dean Fell and others; this and other pieces will doubtless be on view from time to time in the new installation being set up in the Chapter House especially for the display of plate—a treasury that will draw on the resources of all the church plate of the diocese, and (being handsomely subsidised by the Goldsmiths' Company) will show modern smiths' work as well, and be open to visitors. In the Chapter House, note fine carving in capitals and bosses, and four beautifully delicate paintings in the vault.

Christ Church Hall is the largest pre-Victorian hall in either Oxford or Cambridge, and houses on its panelled walls, under a lofty hammerbeam roof, the richest collection of portraits. These could almost constitute a national portrait gallery rather than a collegiate one. Traditionally, the bust of the reigning sovereign (who is the Visitor of Christ Church) presides over the assembly of living dons, canons, students and past alumni, from the centre of the end wall, behind the high table. The bust of Elizabeth II is by Oscar Nemon, and over it hangs a copy of Holbein's enduring, straddling, whole-length image of the founder Henry VIII.

The artistic quality of the portraits tends to improve after the seventeenth century: those of some of the most distinguished early men of the House—Lely's Bishop Fell, Kneller's John Locke —seem to be secondary versions rather than originals, but later the splendid swell of white lawn rochets and judicial wigs and scarlet is answered by some fine painting. There is Gainsborough; Reynolds (Robinson, Archbishop of Armagh); Millais (Gladstone, one of Christ Churchs' many Prime Ministers); and Watts (Dean Liddell). The recent choice of painters has been boldly enterprising and so not always universally approved—Sir William Coldstream's Earl of Avon (Anthony Eden, another Prime Minister) and Graham Sutherland's Dean Simpson. Of C. L. Dodgson, alias Lewis Carroll, there seems unfortunately no worthy portrait: Herkomer's unrevealing head and shoulders of him is posthumous, based on a photograph.

The Library formerly held much of Christ Church's picture collection (other than its institutional portraits). In 1964–67, however, with the aid of a benefaction from Sir Charles Forte

RICARDO FREWEN
MEDICO CELEBERRIMO
ÆDIS CHRISTI ALUMNO

Louis Francois Roubiliac: *Richard Frewen*.
Marble, 1757.

and a remarkably ingenious (and self-effacing) design by the
architects Powell and Moya, Christ Church acknowledged
that its collection of Old Master paintings—and more especially,
drawings—was unique amongst the colleges of Oxford or Cambridge, by building a new gallery specially for it.

The Library (designed by George Clarke, Fellow of All
Souls) is still, however, noteworthy for more than its books.
Apart from the noble serenity of its upper room (finished 1764)
with its superb woodwork and plaster, it retains at the foot of the
stairs a strange cluster, or grove, of marble busts on pedestals.
These include some unexpected masterpieces of the art, surely
vivid enough to convert anyone whom the sight of the bust
normally consumes with a dreadful ennui. Most notable are
Rysbrack's Robert Freind (1738), and Roubiliac's Richard
Frewen (1757): an astonishing characterization, as if of an ancestor

of Mr. Toad of Toad Hall). There is also a group of royal busts, the death of whose sitters has dispossessed them through the years of their traditional place of honour behind the High Table in the Hall: Rysbrack's George I and George II; Bacon's George III; a good version of Chantrey's oft repeated George IV, and Victoria by Thomas Brock. Amongst them, Epstein's bronze of Dean Lowe (1957) strikes a somewhat sombre note. The planner of Peckwater Quad, Dean Aldrich, is recorded by a beautifully direct and fresh marble by a sculptor whose name still eludes identification.

But most impressive of all, in a niche up the staircase is Rysbrack's whole-length commemorative statue of Christ Church's greatest son of the intellect, the philosopher John Locke. The admirably controlled movement of the draperies below that gaunt and spectral profile makes this the most striking of whole-length statues in Oxford, rivalling Roubiliac's *Newton* at Cambridge—both of them noble examples of the eighteenth century's pleasure in celebrating not only royal and military heroes in monumental marble, but also the heroes of human intelligence.

For the paintings and drawings once in the Library, the new Gallery (in Canterbury Quad) is a worthy home. The impetus of the collection and much of the present holdings, come from General John Guise, who became a B.A. from Christ Church in 1701, and died at a ripe old age in 1765. He became a professional soldier, a "character", and a passionate collector of pictures and drawings. As soldier he was extravagantly brave, even if, as sometimes happens with very brave men, rather dottily so. As character he was mildly deplored by Horace Walpole. ("When he is brave enough to perform such actions really as are almost incredible, what pity it is that he should forever persist in saying things that are totally so . . . ."). As collector he was voracious, and when he died he left all his paintings and drawings to Christ Church. The paintings were supplemented by later benefactions notably from W. T. H. Fox-Strangways, later 4th Earl of Ilchester (also a major benefactor to the Ashmolean), in 1828 and 1834; from the writer Walter Savage Landor via his great-nieces in 1897; and most recently from the bequest of Sir Richard Nosworthy (d. 1966). The drawings have hardly been added to at all, though some in the collection came from other earlier sources—notably that Christ Church virtuoso of the arts, Dean Aldrich.

Guise's paintings (about 184 of them) reflect a fairly typical mid-eighteenth-century English taste for the Renaissance, the great Venetians, the *Seicento*, and this taste extended to the buying or commissioning of copies (as for instance the Guise version of Raphael's *Transfiguration*). The tendency of all paintings of a given period to be attributed only to the major masters of that period was even more common then than now, so that paintings

Sir Anthonie Van Dyck: *The Continence of Scipio*. Oil on canvas, 1620/21(?).

that Guise bought as Titians or Leonardos are copies, studio versions or "school of". Others, like the Veronese *Marriage of St. Catherine* or the fine Tintoretto male portrait, are entirely authentic.

Guise was unusual in various ways. He did not subscribe to his English contemporaries' interest in certain styles of Dutch and Flemish painting, nor that for early eighteenth-century masters like Watteau, while his otherwise typical admiration for seventeenth-century Italian masters was qualified by something of a penchant for the low-life side of their work. The outstanding instance of this is also one of the most famous pictures in the collection: the huge, raw, rather jokey-macabre *Butcher's Shop* with its dangling carcases, by Annibale Carracci. But there is something of the same quality in the equally vast *Continence of*

Scipio by Van Dyck—though that is not from Guise. (Do not miss the small, very spirited study of a horseman by Van Dyck, perhaps more to modern taste.)

Upon arriving in Oxford, Guise's pictures were unfortunately handed over to a local restorer, one Bonus; and Bonus, according to Walpole, "entirely repainted them, and as entirely spoiled them". This explains the bruised appearance of many Guise pictures, but many likewise have recently been revealed by judicious cleaning to be in far from ruinous condition. The few paintings by contemporaries of Guise presumably did not need Bonus' attention, and are in splendid condition—for example, the Zuccarelli and the dazzling little *Birth of the Virgin* by the Neapolitan Giaquinto.

The paintings from Fox-Strangways and from Landor both reflect a relatively precocious delight of their collectors for early Italian painting. Excellent examples of Tuscan art before 1400: the monumental little triptych, very close to Duccio; the *Baptist Enthroned;* the enchanting fragment of *Musical Angels.* There is a *Madonna* close enough to Piero della Francesca to retain much of the potency of that serene magic; a lyrical Botticelli studio piece; and Filippino's dream-like, enigmatic *Wounded Centaur.* Fox-Strangway's taste extended further—to Salvator Rosa, and to a fragment of a *Lamentation* now reasonably claimed as an original by Hugo van der Goes.

Landor's taste was unsteadier but often charming—the nine fragments from a Tuscan composite of the *Lives of the Saints, c.*1450, are typical, while Giovanni di Paolo's starkly elegant little *Calvary* would worthily represent Sienese painting in any major gallery in the world. The Nosworthy bequest has added some interesting extensions to the collections: two excellent landscapes by Salvator Rosa, landscapes by Dughet and by Vermeer of Haarlem. Also two eighteenth-century English portraits, to support Reynolds's portrait of General Guise in his old age— pawky, sharp-nosed, sunken-cheeked under his prim grey thatch of a wig.

Christ Church's wealth of institutional portraits is huge, but scattered through the college and not very visible except for the superior constellation that adorn the Hall. In the Picture Gallery, however, you will find one oddity: the strange uncouth portrait of a college scullion, clutching a pewter plate, by John Riley (a very early likeness of a servant, about 1680). You will also find one major masterpiece (if the Senior Common Room is still lending it to the Gallery): Frans Hals's account, small but monumental, of an *Old Woman*, combining bravura and economy in that marvellously direct style of his last works.

The drawings of course cannot be maintained in permanent exhibition—for reasons of conservation, not less than of space—but a changing selection is always on view in a singularly comfortable and agreeable setting (with a bar to lean on). A full

OPPOSITE: Jacopo Tintoretto, after Michelangelo: *Head of Giuliano de' Medici.* Charcoal drawing, touched with white.

Claude Lorrain: *A River in Flood*. Pen and
brush drawing with brown wash,
c. 1630–35.

OPPOSITE: Sir Peter Paul Rubens: *Head of the
Emperor Galba*. Black chalk drawing
touched with white.

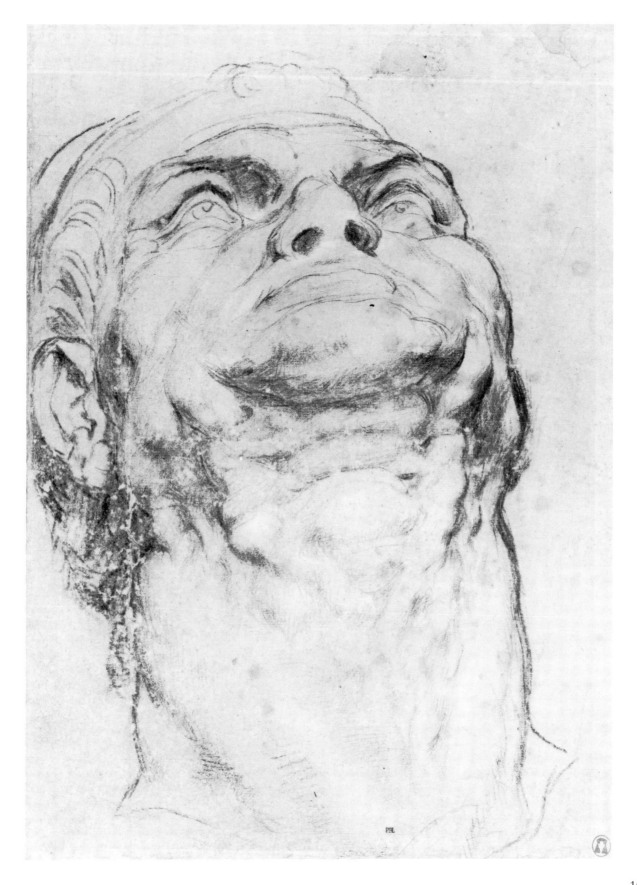

and scholarly index to the complete collection is provided by Mr. J. Byam Shaw's admirable Catalogue (1976) of the drawings. (Mr. Byam Shaw is also responsible for the full 1967 catalogue of *Paintings by Old Masters at Christ Church Oxford*.) The drawings constitute, by any standard, a major collection: they include, for example, works by Raphael, Michelangelo, Leonardo, Correggio, Titian, Tintoretto and Veronese. The most important surviving drawing by Hugo van der Goes, a *Jacob and Raphael*, is there, and the Carracci, Rubens, Van Dyck, Rembrandt and Claude are all represented.

Guise bought not only in England but in France and Italy, and often from the most famous collections that were coming on to the market in his time or not long before it: those of Sir Peter Lely; of Nicholas Laniere (who had bought for Charles I and the Earl of Arundel); of Jonathan Richardson and of Carlo Ridolfi. Together with the Ashmolean collection, the Christ Church drawings make Oxford a major centre of study for anyone interested in Old Master drawings.

Hugo van der Goes: *Jacob and Rachel*. Brush and brown wash drawing, touched with white.

OPPOSITE: Leonardo da Vinci: *Grotesque bust of a Man*. Black chalk drawing, pricked for transfer, 1503–04.

CHAPTER EIGHT

THE COLLEGES

Other than Christ Church

N O OTHER COLLEGE HAS so much quite so accessible to the ordinary visitor as Christ Church, and no other has perhaps quite such a range of treasures. The colleges being primarily the working quarters of dons and students, they have to preserve the seclusion and privacy necessary to enable their work to continue. In fact, all of them do admit visitors, though at restricted and occasionally unpredictable hours, and what is opened does vary a great deal. Individual sets of rooms, whether dons' or undergraduates', are of course private. Common rooms and libraries, where college treasures of one kind or another do tend to accumulate, are normally visitable only by previous arrangement, as they are in constant use by scholars. The halls and chapels, you will with luck find open, and if not open, the porter on the gate or a colleague (obliged perhaps by a small *douceur*) may be able to show them to you. Colleges tend to display in their halls the portraits of their most famous benefactors and alumni. If you wish to be quite certain of being able to see any specific item, the only safe way is to make an appointment in advance.

The following pages offer little more than hints. Mrs. Poole's monumental catalogue, as noted already, provides a working index to Oxford portraits. The Colleges' plate, of great richness, is almost omitted, as it really is invisible (for obvious reasons) to the ordinary visitor, and can only be seen by very special arrangement. The standard account is still H. C. Moffatt's *Old Oxford Plate* (1908) though monographs on several individual college collections have been published or are under way. The best summary of chapel furnishings is in Pevsner's *Oxfordshire* (1975: Buildings of England series), and includes a special section on pre-nineteenth-century stained glass by Peter A. Newton.

IX. AGNOLO BRONZINO *Don Garzia de' Medici*. Panel, *c.* 1560.

X. CLAUDE LORRAIN *Landscape with Ascanius Shooting the Stag.*
Canvas, 1682.

XI. NICOLAS POUSSIN *The Exposition of Moses.* Canvas, 1654.

XII. GIOVANNI BELLINI *St. Jerome in the Desert*. Panel.

XIII. BICCI DI LORENZO *St. Nicholas Rebuking the Tempest*. Panel, 1433.

XIV. FRANS HALS *Seated Woman*. Oil on panel, *c.* 1660(?).

XV. THOMAS GAINSBOROUGH *Miss Gainsborough Gleaning*. Canvas (unfinished), *c.* 1760.

XVI. CAMILLE PISSARRO *Vue de ma fenêtre, Eragny*. Oil on canvas, 1888.

XVII. J. M. W. TURNER *A View of Worcester College*. Watercolour, 1804(?).

XVIII. ARTHUR HUGHES *Home from Sea (A Mother's Grave)*. Canvas, 1863.

XIX. HENRI DE TOULOUSE-LAUTREC *La Toilette (Celui qui se peigne).*
    Oil on millboard, 1891.

The following notes are set out in alphabetical order of colleges, for convenience, but the more recent foundations are grouped together at the end of the chapter.

ALL SOULS was founded by Archbishop Chichele and King Henry VI, in 1438, though the statues (and a relief of the Resurrection), on the Gate Tower, are replacements by W. C. H. King, 1948. The originals, of the mid-fifteenth century, are in the undercroft to the Chapel, and still tell, battered though they are, of very high quality. The Chapel, though consecrated in 1442, is overall transposed into somewhat nineteenth-century mood by Scott's restoration of 1872–6. Thus the vast and complex reredos is original (1447), but the figures—over thirty of them—are by E. C. Geflowski in 1872. The preservation of the framework is precious and rare enough; it was concealed for many years by a huge painting of the *Last Judgment* by Isaac Fuller (about 1664), now vanished, though related fragments kept in the college survive—they are bold in handling, fairly coarse, and most would agree the recovery of the reredos was a gain. (The altar piece, before Scott's restoration, was a large and important *Noli me Tangere* by Mengs, now deposited in the Ashmolean Museum.) The glass in the antechapel is of good quality, and much of it original, of the decade 1440–50. Co-founder Chichele features among the saints north of the great west window but apparently not co-founder Henry VI. The memorials include some good brasses, and otherwise most notably the monument to Robert Havenden (d. 1614) in that characteristic academic attitude of avowing mortality with a skull, denying it with a book. A grandish monument to Dr. George Clarke (designer of the library at Christ Church, d. 1736) has an appropriate architectural background. Sir William Anson has as memorial one of those startling pale full-length recumbent effigies, rather late in the effigy revival (1914: by John Tweed).

In the north quad there is a fine sundial of 1658, restored in the eighteenth century. Christopher Wren was Bursar of the college at this date, so the sundial may be one of his early works. Those splendid iron gates, through which the passer-by glimpses from Radcliffe Square such secluded academic magic, were designed by Hawksmoor in the early 1730's. In the Codrington Library beyond, the woodwork design was Hawksmoor's but modified by James Gibbs: along the cornices of the gallery shelving is ranged a sequence of twenty-four lead portrait busts. These comprise a retrospective survey of distinguished Fellows, all provided about 1750–6 by the then-fashionable sculptor (and a great Oxford favourite), Sir Henry Cheere. They go back to characters like the great physician Linacre (d. 1524) or Elizabeth I's Secretary of State, Sir William Petre, but come more nearly up to the time of their making with Fellows like Wren and Clarke. They are slightly unusual in that the subjects of such series of busts—a common form of library adornments at this period—tended to be great literary figures. The statue of Codring-

Sir Henry Cheere: *Christopher Codrington*.
Marble, *c.* 1734.

ton, the benefactor of the library—full length, high on his plinth at the hub of the library, clad in Roman military gear yet with a pile of books at his feet—is also by Cheere. Like General Guise at Christ Church, Codrington was a benefactor with an appealing mixture of the military and the scholarly; also a typical example, as portrayed here, of the extension of the practise of setting up life-size statues from royalty to other ranks. At the far end of the library, likewise life-size in marble (though seated) there is that formidable lawyer Sir William Blackstone (d. 1780), by John Bacon. Massive in his judge's robes, displaying his celebrated *Commentaries*, he rather than Codrington presides over the Library with virile authority. (The judge's admonishing finger is said to be a recent replacement, by Firth, having been snapped in a college romp). Elsewhere in the College, there is Roubiliac's long-posthumous (1751) evocation in marble of Chichele, already mentioned. Also there is another bust of extraordinary quality, Cheere's plaster of the architect, Nicholas Hawksmoor, frankly and sourly stating its subject as a Roman and, as far as is known, the only portrait ever made of him. (A modern bronze cast from it is in the National Portrait Gallery.) In the Hall, paintings of Chichele, Henry VI, Christopher Wren, and others. The windows have portraits, by Powell, of the six Worthies of All Souls: Wren, Codrington, Lord Talbot of Hensol, Blackstone, Heber and Lord Salisbury. The most celebrated piece of plate is the "giant" salt (fifteenth century, and by tradition connected with the Founder) borne aloft on the head of a walking bearded man. The College owns remarkable architectural drawings.

BALLIOL was chartered in 1282, but is now of pronouncedly Victorian character. In the Chapel (1856–7, by Butterfield) there are some survivors: a pulpit of the 1630s, and a very handsome crowned eagle lectern, given also in the 1630s. Reset in the windows there is a quantity of old glass, mainly early sixteenth century from the former chapel, but the most remarkable object is the strange conceit of a miniature recumbent effigy, by Onslow Ford, of Balliol's most celebrated Master, Benjamin Jowett (d. 1893). Jowett was small in stature, and this sculpture, almost toy-like in scale but very rich in its mixed materials, stone, bronze, and mosaic (cf. the same sculptor's Shelley memorial in University College), conveys both dignity and pathos.

The Library (remodelled by Wyatt, 1792–4) has Gothicky bookcases, but a nice clumsy sculpture of St. Catherine and angels of *c.* 1635–40. The holdings of the Library include some well-known early manuscripts; there are also Robert Browning manuscripts.

Holywell Manor in Manor Road is also part of Balliol, and has a room painted by Gilbert Spencer, here rivalling his brother Stanley in style, with an account of John of Balliol's life. In the quad is a fountain by Peter Lyon.

BRASENOSE was founded in 1509, but was preceded by Brasenose Hall.

What is believed to be the original *Brazen-nose* door knocker is now in the College hall, and who would disbelieve the story that students, migrating from Oxford to Stamford after an unpleasant riot in 1383, had taken it with them; that in 1890 the College had bought a house in Stamford where the Nose then was, simply to recover the knocker (and in 1930 sold the house at a profit)? Over the entrance to the Hall, three weather-beaten busts dating from 1636—said to be of the Founders, William Smythe, Bishop of Lincoln and Sir Richard Sutton in 1509, and Alfred the Great (or, some suggest, Johannes Erigena, said to have lectured on this spot in the *ninth* century). Portraits include King Alfred (1769, by Edward Penny); the Founder; a rare lady—Joyce Frankland, 1586, holding her Nuremberg watch (a copy of a contemporary version elsewhere in the College);

a Tilly Kettle of Francis Yarborough, 1763; and a Hoppner of William Cleaver, *c*. 1800.

In the splendid Chapel (Gothic revival of *c*. 1665) are a good, very large brass eagle lectern given in 1731 and chandeliers of 1749. The glass in the west windows is unusual, from designs by J. R. Mortimer, 1776. The monuments include James Smith by R. Westmacott the Younger, 1838, a timeless very pale profile; a very early Eric Gill (1905) for Sir Albert Watson; but perhaps most notably Sir W. B. Richmond's bronze plaque for the famous aesthete and historian of the Renaissance, Walter Pater, which includes not only a medallion of Pater, but attendant ones of Plato, Dante, Leonardo and Michelangelo, all amongst a spreading willow.

The College is rich in seventeenth-century silver, but has further what are believed to be the only mediaeval pair of Chalices (1498–9) surviving. These are associated with the Founder, Bishop Smyth.

CORPUS CHRISTI was founded in 1519. In the front quad stands the celebrated sundial, with the College's symbolic pelican. This goes back to 1581, though it has been amended and added to since—the pelican itself is a recent replacement by Michael Black. The statue of the Founder Bishop Fox of Winchester, facing the gateway, is of 1819 or later. The original of John Corvus's magnificently hieratic portrait of Fox is probably the one now hung in the Hall, but the College owns several versions. In the Hall under that fine hammerbeam roof, Fox's companions include good contemporary academic portraits of two early nineteenth-century bishops, copious with lawn: Thomas Burgess, by W. Owen, 1819, as Bishop of St. David's; and Edward Coplestone, with St. Paul's in the background but apparently when Bishop of Llandaff, attributed to Sir M. A. Shee. Also here are two eminent lawyers, Lord Stowell by T. Phillips, 1827, and Lord Tenterden, by W. Owen, 1819, both fully bewigged and robed.

The Chapel has some furnishings of about 1677—stalls, reredos, and perhaps the screen—but the brass eagle lectern, given before 1537, is claimed as the only pre-Reformation one in Oxford. The altar painting, an *Adoration of the Shepherds*, is close to Rubens if not by him. But the most celebrated treasure of the College is its plate, especially those pieces associated with the Founder, which the College managed to preserve from the Royalist mint in the Civil War—Fox's Pastoral Staff with the pelican in its piety and St. Peter with his key (for Exeter Cathedral), and saints, all wrought with marvellous delicate intricacy up into the loop of the crozier. This is one of the finest pieces of early Tudor goldsmith's work to have survived. Also Fox's hour-glass-shaped standing salt, his chalice and paten (these very rare, in gold); two flagons, two superb rosewater dishes, and then there are spoons, a font cup and cover, and so on.

EXETER was founded in 1314, but internally it is now dominated by Sir Giles Gilbert Scott's chapel of 1856–9. Flanking its doorway are retrospective statues of the first and second Founders, Bishop Stapledon (1314) and Sir William Petre (1565). The Chapel is all of a piece, rich Victorian, featuring work of standard top specialist craftsmen: stalls by Bodley, 1884; iron and brass gates by Skidmore of Coventry; a great deal of the stone carving by J. Birnie Philip; mosaics by Salviati; glass by Clayton and Bell. There are some attractive early Italian panels of saints, but the real single showpiece is the Morris tapestry, *Adoration of the Magi*, designed by Burne-Jones, 1887–90. Burne-Jones and Morris had been undergraduates at Exeter about the time the Chapel started building. It is one of Burne-Jones's most haunting and most sombre designs, long figures still amongst the lilies.

In the Hall hangs a pious assembly of Founders or benefactors. The dour Sir William Petre is a good and typical Elizabethan image, probably by or after Steven van der Meulen. A vastly splendiferous whole-length retrospective evocation of the Founder, Stapledon, is probably the masterpiece of its painter, the Rev. Matthew William Peters, R.A., who presented it in 1780. The portraits proceed through the generations to a pinched image, very sharp, of the late Rector Barber, by Pietro Annigoni.

In the Margary Quad is an abstract sculpture by Jose de Alberdi, 1968.

HERTFORD has a broken history. Once Hart Hall, it was founded in 1284, but subject thereafter to various dislocations until 1874. Architecturally Hertford is unified by the work of that ubiquitous Oxford architect, Sir Thomas G. Jackson, 1887–1914. His Chapel has its devotees; the reredos is a crucifixion carved in 1919 by Sir G. Frampton. (Jackson is best known for his great contribution to Oxford, the Bridge of Sighs over New College Lane—not so much architecture, more a piece of corny picturesque and as such marvellously successful.) Over a door in the old Octagon Chapel is a rare survivor of an earlier period, a modest, battered but still charming carved relief of the Annunciation, perhaps about 1520.

JESUS was founded by Hugh Price, 1571, though judging by the number of portraits the credit goes to Elizabeth I. Price's portrait is in the Hall, a tidy small Elizabethan (a copy of Vertue's engraving of this, 1739, used to be given to every scholar of the College); also in the Hall is a bronze bust of Elizabeth I, of uncertain date. The large whole-length painting of her, given in 1686–7 (related to one at Trinity College, Cambridge, but with attendant angels added perhaps by the painter mayor of Oxford, John Taylor) has been replaced by the finest Elizabeth in the College, an admirable half-length of 1590 with rather floral attributes (holding a thistle, and featuring roses, strawberries and ferns). In the Hall also there hang a version of Van Dyck's state portrait of Charles I; the benefactor Sir Leiline Jenkins, painted by the rare Dutch artist

Herbert Tuart, 1679; and, somewhat unexpectedly, a fine Sir Thomas Lawrence of the great Regency architect, John Nash, 1827. (He asked for his portrait to be painted for the College instead of his being paid a fee.)

Elsewhere in the College are some curious pictures—a lady with a monkey, suspected by some to be a cleaning lady, Goody Asaph, c.1650; one of the most characteristic of all Pre-Raphaelite portraits, Holman Hunt's Canon Jenkins, 1852 (the College also has a drawing for this). In the Chapel is a memorial to Sir Eubule Thelwall, Principal 1621–30 and a great builder; angels draw back curtains showing him kneeling with an open book. Here also a replica of Kennington's bust of T. E. Lawrence in St. Paul's.

KEBLE is high Victorian religion, the Oxford Movement expressed in red brick. Butterfield's Chapel (1856–82) is the cult object, indeed one of the most startling objects on the Oxford scene, an Anglican temple such as Lucifer might have built before his fall but suspecting something was nigh and defying it. Furniture and decorations were all controlled by Butterfield—glass, by A. Gibbs; reredos, pulpit and lectern. What most people go to see is in a small side chapel added in 1892, Holman Hunt's *Light of the World*, showing Christ with a lantern knocking at a closed door. ("Behold, I stand at the door and knock. . . .") Painted in 1851–3, it was given by Mrs. Combe to Keble in 1873. The version in St. Paul's Cathedral is much later (1900), and painted, according to some, in pique because Keble was then charging the public to see the first version. Once known to thousands, perhaps millions, in reproduction, the image has provoked superlative admiration and superlative scorn. Carlyle: "a mere papistical phantasy". Ruskin: "one of the very noblest works of sacred art produced in this or any other age. . . ." It was begun at night "with the phosphor light of a perfect moon"; later stages involved candles, even gas. Among those who posed for the head of Christ were Christina Rossetti and Elizabeth Siddal. Also, in the Inner Chapel, is a *Descent from the Cross*, ascribed to the Flemish Mannerist Marten de Vos. In the Library are busts of Newman, by T. Woolner, and of Pusey and Keble (both by George Richmond). The Hall has portraits of benefactors and Wardens, as usual; but also, deposited on indefinite loan by the Tate Gallery, a splendid mythological scene by G. F. Watts.

LINCOLN celebrates its Founders in its Hall. Retrospective portraits of the first Founder (1427), Richard Fleming, Bishop of Lincoln, and the second Founder (1427), Richard Fleming, Bishop of Lincoln and later Archbishop of York, are of c. 1638 and both probably by Richard Greenbury. Also in the Hall is John William's portrait of Lincoln's most famous Fellow, John Wesley, about 1743: hands folded on a volume lettered *Homilies 2*, with a Bible alongside; the hands are calm, but the face, with rather thrusting lower lip, is eloquent of determination. Also a portrait of

OPPOSITE: William Holman Hunt: *The Light of the World*. Oil on canvas, 1853. "Behold, I stand at the door and knock".

Mark Pattison, famous writer and sometime Rector, posthumous (by A. Macdonald, 1900), and one of Lord Morley by John Collier, 1913.

The Chapel (1629–31) is rich in woodwork of various dates in the seventeenth century, especially the stalls with their carved statuettes. The glass is firmly attributed to Bernard van Linge, around 1629–31. The east window shows illustrations to the Old and New Testaments; the other windows have the twelve apostles (south), matched by twelve prophets (north). The pulpit from which Wesley preached is still there, and his room (restored with donations from American Methodists) has relics where once the "Holy Club" met: a memorial bust presides over the first quadrangle.

Since 1975 Lincoln has incorporated the former All Saints (City Church), which it has brilliantly adapted for use as college library.

MAGDALEN was one of the foundations, in 1458, of Bishop Waynflete, but the Chapel of 1474–80 was restored 1829–34 and the stone screen and elaborate reredos is of that date, though the copious statues on the latter were added in about 1865. The chantry to the north was meant for the Founder, Bishop Waynflete, but houses instead the tomb of his father, Richard Patten *c.* 1450, translated from Wainfleet in 1833. (The Founder and his brother are in miniature beside the effigy's pillow.) Furnishings and monuments are fairly rich. In the antechapel, John and Thomas Lyttleton, brothers drowned in 1635, by Nicholas Stone. More typical are Laurence Humphrey, d. 1590,—academic divine with book; William Layton, d. 1624, same theme with skull added, and allegorical figures. A brass eagle lectern is of 1633, and two sculptures on the *Noli me Tangere* theme are by Sir F. Chantrey, about the time of the Chapel's restoration, and by David Wynne (in bronze), 1963. The altarpiece is seventeenth-century Spanish, *Christ Carrying the Cross*. There is a Burne-Jones drawing of Mary Magdalen washing Christ's feet, and (on loan) a small Boilly painting, *trompe l'oeil*, of an ivory crucifix. In the antechapel some old stalls reward a close look, for they have crispish misericords. The blue-green and gold cope is fifteenth century and described in the Founder's will (his stockings and buskins also are elsewhere in the College). On the buttresses of the cloister is a guardian array of remarkably ingenious and picturesque gargoyles apparently by John Butt and Robert Carver.

The Hall has original linenfold panelling (said to have come from Reading Abbey at the time of the dissolution of the monasteries), and also a sequence of elaborate carved panels with Renaissance motifs, one dated 1541, one featuring King Henry VIII, and others scenes from the story of St. Mary Magdalene. Portraits include those of the Founder; of Bishop Fox; of Charles I's brother, Henry Prince of Wales; of the romantic Royalist cavalry general Prince Rupert (a robust whole-length by J. M.

Wright); of Bishop Hough (who assisted James II's imposition on the College of a Roman Catholic President); and of the Venerable Dr. Routh (by H. W. Pickersgill) who reigned as President from 1791 to 1854. Magdalen has a rich library and fine plate, and elsewhere in the College are rarities like the winged genie with the human head, a relief from Nimrod *c.* 860 B.C. similar to that in the Ashmolean, and some venerable tapestries, early sixteenth century, one of which is thought to represent the betrothal of Prince Arthur and Catherine of Aragon.

MERTON goes back to about 1262, and has prospered. The gateway from Merton Street into Front Quad is of 1418, with original star vaulting with bosses and a tympanum showing St. John the Baptist and Christ in the Wilderness. (Statues of the Founder, Walter de Merton, and of Henry III are replacements.) The gateway from the Front Quad into Fellows' Quad (1497) again has a fine vault with very spirited bosses of signs of the zodiac. In the Hall are portraits of the Founder (retrospective, given 1796) and of the philosopher Duns Scotus (d. 1308, even more retrospective); of Bodley (copy), and a sombre range of nineteenth-century college worthies including Bishop Mandell Creighton by Herkomer. (Elsewhere in the College there are a number of clear-cut sensitive head-and-shoulders in small, by a rare but remarkable eighteenth-century painter of Huguenot stock, Lewis Vaslet).

The extremely grand (though unfinished) Chapel is appropriately rich in fittings and furnishings. The extraordinary font, exotically of Siberian green marble almost as if a monster work by Fabergé, was given by Tsar Alexander in 1816 (there is also a more usual one, designed by Butterfield, 1851). Also a fine seventeenth-century screen, and a superb brass lectern of about 1500. The imaginary progression into the never-built nave is via a colossal *trompe l'oeil* painting by Harker Studios, 1968: there was going to be a portrait group at ground level, but the College disapproved, and that bit now is in Dorchester Abbey. The more usual altarpiece is a good Tintorettesque *Crucifixion*. The monuments include a number of brasses; a cartouche, modest in scale but rich in sentiment, for the archetypal Oxford antiquary, Anthony à Wood, who died in 1695; and a severe monument by the Pre-Raphaelite sculptor, Woolner, to Coleridge Patteson (d. 1871). The finest memorials are of two great Oxford benefactors and erstwhile friends: Sir Thomas Bodley, died 1613, by Nicholas Stone, and Sir Henry Savile, died 1622. Their busts face each other along the length of the transepts. Bodley is attended by the figures of Music, Arithmetic, Grammar and Rhetoric; Savile has statuettes of St John Chrysostom, Ptolemy, Euclid and Tacitus; and over all is Fame. Below, paintings of Eton and of Merton are incorporated. Two statues on the Merton Street exterior, of the Virgin and St John the Baptist, are much weathered, but of quality. Much of the glass is of perhaps as early as 1289, and still *in situ*; the donor was Henry de Mamesfeld who died in 1328. Most of the fifteenth-century glass in the transepts has gone, though some very fine figures thence are re-set in the east windows of the choir. Further remains of the glass of that period are to be found in the Old Library, which retains its characteristic Jacobean library furnishings. The college plate is very rich in post-Restoration silver.

NEW COLLEGE was founded by William of Wykeham in 1379. At the New College Lane entrance it has the oldest of Oxford's gate-houses (*c*. 1380) and, high on it, the Virgin with figures of an angel and the kneeling Founder. In the Quad (Great Quad) the Muniment Tower repeats these three figures. The Chapel is both very large and richly furnished. And very variously so: a startling confrontation is provided by a nervously animated *St James*, by El Greco, opposite a stiff Sampson Strong painting of the Founder, with the latter's crozier, exquisite goldsmith's work, enshrined in a glazed niche. The very copious reredos is of Gilbert Scott's restoration, 1877–81. Five tiers of figures by Pearson rise above sculptured reliefs by Westmacott (fragments of the fourteenth-century reredos survive and are kept in the Music Room). In the stalls, however, much fourteenth-century work survives, especially in a series of some thirty-eight very spirited misericords. The windows are eighteenth-century and rather harsh, by William Price (south) and Peckitt of York (north). In the antechapel, all the windows except one are of *c*. 1385; the exception is the west window, painted 1778–85 by Thomas Jarvis to designs by Sir Joshua Reynolds, a *Nativity* with the *Seven Virtues* below. This has had a poor press—"washy", thought Horace Walpole—but their clear colour and graceful elegance begin perhaps to attract more grateful attention now. The antechapel also has a considerable array of brasses, mainly fifteenth-century, the finest a large one of Thomas Cranley; high on the bosses are lively carved heads that some claim as very early attempts at naturalistic portraiture. There are good monuments too: among them a very finely individualised version of the academic-divine-with-book theme, Hugh Barker by Nicholas Stone, 1632, almost quivering with apprehension; and war memorials by Eric Gill. But also, on the main axis by the closed west door, the astounding figure of *Lazarus* embattled with his grave clothes, by Epstein, seven feet high. Two largish panels of an Annunciation are ascribed to Montagna. The Founder's gloves and mitre may also be visible, but New College seems now to have established the happy practice of showing many of the most important pieces from its Treasury in an open exhibition through the summer vacation; a representation of the extraordinary splendid late-mediaeval plate—the Hourglass salt, perhaps, or the grotesque Monkey salt; Archbishop Warham's celadon bowl; the Warden's Grace Cup, about 1480; a Pax of about 1520; and also admirable later pieces. Then there will be items from the

El Greco: *Apostle* (St. James the Great). Oil on canvas, *c*. 1610.

very rich library—the great mid-thirteenth-century Psalter, its illuminations by W. de Brailes heavy with gold. And relics—the so-called "unicorn's" horn (actually narwhal's) that Elizabeth I's favourite, the Earl of Leicester, coveted. (The College gave him the tip but retained the rest.)

In the Cloisters are eight venerable and weather-beaten statues, removed for safety reasons from the tower of St. Mary's, the University church. They were probably fourteenth-century additions to the tower (*c*. 1280). Others from the same source are at All Souls. In the Hall, a fairly dense array of portraits, including retrospective ones of the Founder, Archbishop Warham (after Holbein). and College worthies up to (and beyond) the celebrated Warden Spooner, immortal begetter of the spoonerism. Others elsewhere in the College include a Romney of John Oglander, and the great wit Sydney Smith, by E. U. Eddis. If proceeding to the beautiful gardens, do not miss the wrought-iron screen (by Thomas Robinson, 1711). By the new Sacher building (1942, Roberts and Clarke) is a bronze by Barbara Hepworth.

ORIEL goes back to 1326. Over the porch of the Hall, rather anonymous statues are of Edward II (who gave the College its statute) and Charles I (or James I, or even Edward III), with one of the Virgin above. Portraits in the Hall include (very retro-spective) a whole-length of Edward II, signed and dated by Thomas Hudson, 1753, and another of the Duke of Beaufort signed by the Venetian painter Soldi, 1748; the portrait of Rhodes is by Tenny-son Cole, and that of Thomas Hughes (of *Tom Brown's Schooldays*) by Lowes C. Dickinson. Elsewhere are portraits of Newman (by Ouless), John Eveleigh (a fine Hoppner), Matthew Arnold (by Lowes Dickinson), and others: also a painting ascribed to Vasari of the Italian ports. The chapel has good seventeenth-century woodwork, with a wooden lectern dated 1654; a window (southwest) by William Peckitt, of the *Presentation in the Temple*. But most remarkable here is a part of a very fine altarpiece, given in 1911 by Alfred Stowe, by the Fleming Bernard van Orley (1491/2–1542): *Christ bearing the Cross*. (A companion piece is in the National Gallery of Scotland.) Oriel's portraits have recently been enhanced, as noted already, by a remarkable gift from Sir Weldon Dalrymple-Champneys of his family portraits together with a new room to house them—an unusually decorative en-semble. The architect who built the Rhodes Building, 1908–11, was of that family (Basil Champneys), and its pompous front on the High is copiously adorned with portrait statues, ranging from that of the Founder Adam de Brome (d. 1332) through Cardinal Newman, Edward VII and George V (rather uncomfortable in trunk hose). Oriel's plate is rich in late seventeenth and eighteenth-century work, with one vast hundred-ounce tankard of 1678–9; but also early pieces, including a gilt beaker associated with Edward, Prince of Wales.

PEMBROKE was founded in 1624. It has some fine portraits,

OPPOSITE: Sir Jacob Epstein: *Lazarus*. Hoptonwood stone, 1948.

such as an admirable late Lawrence of Sir Thomas le Breton (about 1826), but it is primarily, for the non-Oxford man, a point of pilgrimage for the aura of its most famous alumnus, Samuel Johnson. Here are Johnson's teapot, and other relics; a fair version of Reynolds's last portrait of the Doctor, the original of which belonged to Mrs. Thrale, and perhaps the best version of Nollekens' bust of him, 1777. (Johnson objected because Nollekens had insisted that poets had lots of hair and, as Johnson was somewhat lacking, supplied him in his bust with someone else's.)

THE QUEEN'S COLLEGE, though founded in 1340, is physically the most classico-baroque of Oxford college buildings, and as such, excellently accented by statuary: on the gate under the umbrella of the dome, Queen Caroline is by Sir Henry Cheere as are the figures (Law, Physic and Poetry) on the east pediment of the screen on the High. Those on the west pediment are modern replacements: very pretty pompous *putti* with cartouches in the pediments. More full-length statuary along the garden front of the library—Henrietta Maria, Sir Joseph Williamson, Bishop Barlow, Archbishop Lamplugh, Robert Eglesfield, Edward III, Queen Philippa and Charles I—all by an obscure and not exciting sculptor called J. Vanderstein. Externally the Library has further figure carving in the pediments, and inside among the successfully lavish decor of its furnishings and plasterwork (by James Hands, 1695, and Thomas Roberts, 1756) a further statue of Queen Philippa, in wood and perhaps of the early seventeenth century. Plate is rich, including most famously the drinking horn traditionally given by the Founder and inscribed WACCEYL; this was restored in the seventeenth century. In the very grand Chapel, the apse ceiling is by the finest of English baroque painters, Sir James Thornhill (begun 1716); the woodwork and metalwork are mostly of the same period and of high quality. The lectern is earlier, 1662, and signed William Burroghes.

In the Hall, there are retrospective baroque-ified whole-lengths of the Founder, Robert Eglesfield (d. 1349) and of his patron, Queen Philippa, by Thomas Murray, 1695. Others include the great Augustan essayist and poet, Addison by Simon du Bois, and Edmund Gibson by J. Vanderbank. Elsewhere, a fine Rysbrack terracotta of Richard Miller, 1726–7, (once wrongly identified as Wren); a painting of Edmund Halley (the astronomer of the comet) by T. Murray, about 1721, and a burly version of a self-portrait, by the late seventeenth-century painter Isaac Fuller.

In No 33 High Street, annexed to the College, as Drawda Hall, there is some decoration in a Pre-Raphaelite manner done for C. J. Faulkner, a partner of Morris, and perhaps by Swan who worked at the Union.

ST. EDMUND HALL goes back to the early fourteenth century. The Chapel has early glass from Morris and Co., 1865, mainly from Burne-Jones designs, though the *Man of Galilee* and the

Maries at the Sepulchre are Morris's own, and decorative detail is by Philip Webb. Unexpected and very striking is Ceri Richards' forceful altarpiece, *Christ at Emmaeus*, 1957–8; there is a little early seventeenth-century Netherlandish triptych also. The woodwork is all of the 1680s. The former church of St. Peter-in-the-East is now adapted to serve as College library: once Saxon, it now shows evidence of most periods of the Middle Ages, from the early twelfth century onwards.

ST. JOHN'S developed from a Cistercian foundation (first called St. Bernard's) of 1437. The re-foundation, as St. John's, was by Sir Thomas White in 1555. In the tower, over the main entrance from St. Giles, stands the original statue of St. Bernard, perhaps late fifteenth century; but inside on to Front Quad, is his surprising twentieth-century counterpart—Eric Gill's statue of St. John, 1935. The Chapel interior is nineteenth century, but earlier furnishings include an unusual lectern (the eagle has a garland of flowers) of 1733, and a handsome complement of memorials. A few pieces of early embroidery are shown too, representative of the College's rich collection of vestments from the fifteenth to the seventeenth century. In the Hall, amongst the portraits (including Archbishops Laud and Juxon, and George III) there is a scagliola picture, St. John the Baptist after Raphael, by Lamberto Gorio. This very rich foundation has a wealth of portraits, and also some tapestries, distributed through the College. Canterbury Quad, finished in 1636 by Archbishop Laud, has rich decoration eloquent of his lavish taste; he commissioned, from Le Sueur, the bronze statues of Charles I and Henrietta Maria that confront each other across the Quad (1633). The lavish stone carving is mostly by Nicholas Stone's assistants Anthony Gore and Henry Acres—busts of the Virtues and Liberal Arts prominent in the spandrels of the arches. The college owns a bronze bust of Laud himself by Le Sueur (a non-royal bust is a considerable rarity at that date), and the Old Library has (besides some splendid early seventeenth-century heraldic glass) one of his bookcases, and others from as early as 1596. Plate is rich and copious, mainly post-Restoration.

TRINITY The Chapel (1691–4) is one of the most exquisite delights that Oxford can offer. Since that industrious traveller Celia Fiennes noted it in 1694–5 as "wanscoated with walnut-tree and the fine sweet wood . . . just like that at Windsor, it being the same hand", the harvest of ravishing carving that decorates it has been confidently ascribed to Grinling Gibbons. In fact, others may have played some part, but the finest of the decoration, such as that above the altar, is surely the best of Gibbons himself. The Founder's monument (recumbent effigies, Sir Thomas and Lady Pope, the only such in Oxford) is earlier, *c.* 1567, but rather discreetly tucked away. The ceiling paintings, with an *Ascension*, are by Pierre Berchet. Elsewhere to be noted are the very fine iron gates, those on to Parks Road of 1713,

127

those on to the Broad of 1737 but copied from the others. The Gate Tower (Front Quad) has statues of Geometry, Astronomy, Theology and Medicine (of the same date as the Chapel, *c.* 1694). The Old Library has a statue of the Founder over the door, and a good painting of him within, with other college portraits including Cardinal Newman, Lord Goddard, Bishop Percival and others. Cardinal Newman is commemorated again in a bronze bust at the left of the entrance to the Garden (near his former rooms). The plate includes the Founder's Chalice and Paten, gilt, 1527–8, preserved from the great seventeenth-century melting, and a rich holding of post-Restoration plate.

UNIVERSITY COLLEGE has its real origins in a bequest from William of Durham, who died in 1249. About 1700 the College replaced the statue of King Alfred on the gate of the tower of its Front Quad with one of Queen Anne. The wrecked King Alfred stands rather forlorn in the Master's Garden—the legendary claim of the College to have been founded by him is, as remarked by the Regius Professor of Modern History, "though allowed by courtesy, not pressed in argument". The statue of deposed James II (1687) remains—in harmony at last with Queen Anne, his daughter. Alfred is re-asserted in a medallion portrait, about 1904, in the chimney piece of the Hall. Around him are portraits of the other heroes of the college, including Dr. Radcliffe, Dean Stanley, Elizabeth I's Earl of Leicester, and Prime Minister Lord Attlee. Radcliffe, that great Oxford benefactor, occurs in a life-size lead statue (by Francis Bird, 1717) facing on to the Quad named after him: a statue of Queen Mary corresponds on the street side. The Library has rather pompous statues of Lords Eldon and Stowell (designed by M. L. Watson and rejected for Westminster Abbey), but also a lively bust of King Alfred, by that able sculptor Joseph Wilton. In the Chapel there is the most copious surviving work in Oxford of the glass-designer Abraham van Linge: nine windows of 1641, coarse perhaps but bold and full of vigour, with a famous one of Jonah being spewed up by the whale. Also here, in marked stylistic contrast, are several excellent monuments from the hand of the finest English neo-classic sculptor, John Flaxman, especially to the great pioneer of Hindu studies, Sir William Jones (1794), featuring Hindus, lyres, gourds, and Indian musical instruments.

The most celebrated object in University College is the Shelley Memorial, set up in 1893. The drowned poet, pale as death in marble, spread supine on a coloured base that incorporates the bronze muse of poetry. Like the statues of the Lawyers in the library, it is not where it was meant to be (destined for the Protestant cemetery in Rome originally), and Oxford of course had dispensed with the unwanted presence of Shelley himself as undergraduate. Long despised, it now attracts frequent if sometimes unwilling admiration, and is perhaps (though the Jowett memorial in Balliol rivals it) the masterpiece of its sculptor, Onslow Ford.

WADHAM is unusual in its "one-of-a-pieceness", built almost all together in 1610–13, and salutes its Founders, Nicholas and Dorothy Wadham, with statues in the frontispiece in the Front Quad (replacements after the originals by John Blackshaw), with James I above. The Hall has many portraits, and the Chapel excellent seventeenth-century furnishings; the windows include one signed B. van Linge, 1622. The plate includes two fine Elizabethan flagons of 1598–9—the Foundress's, as also her Chalice and Paten cover of 1612–13. The portraiture of College worthies is to be increased by a sculpture of Sir Maurice Bowra, monumental but emergent in rather ectoplasmic style from the back of an armchair.

WORCESTER was originally Gloucester College of about 1283, and retains early mediaeval features, but the Chapel, remodelled by William Burges from 1864, is obligatory for pilgrims along the High-Victorian route. Pevsner notes the floor design as "Early Christian" and statues, lectern, and candlesticks (by W. G. Nicholl) as "in a pure Quattrocento". The stained glass (and ceiling paintings) are by Henry Holiday. In the gardens lurk two from the original set of heads of Emperors outside the Sheldonian, hoary and ghostly with age and decrepitude. But also, elsewhere in the College, there are some interesting portraits —a very rare image of the poet Richard Lovelace, for example, and a marble bust of De Quincey, author and opium-eater, by Steele (the same type as the plaster in the National Portrait Gallery). And, unexpectedly, one of the most gravely grand (and I think the largest) Ruysdael landscapes in Britain. Worcester also owns a remarkable series of architectural drawings, the nucleus being George Clarke's, starting with Inigo Jones but proceeding now through to Burges.

RECENT FOUNDATIONS

Naturally, the newer colleges and comparable institutions have not accumulated treasures to the extent that many of the old foundations have, but several are far from impoverished in detail. The women's colleges' halls tend to be interesting to the historian of portraits not only for the subjects of the paintings, but as extensive witness of gallant attempts to reconcile feminine grace and elegance with the formality of the institutional icon. LADY MARGARET HALL has benefited by an admirable bequest of a collection of twentieth-century British paintings, including Stanley Spencer, David Jones and Christopher Wood; the college Chapel has a beautiful early Burne-Jones triptych, c. 1863, of the Nativity—also an Italian Trecento Flagellation, and a cast of the Torrigiano effigy of Lady Margaret in Westminster Abbey. ST ANNE'S COLLEGE is also fortunate in a collection of modern British paintings (Duncan Grant, Paul Nash).

Among the men's colleges, ST CATHERINE'S is celebrated for its all-of-a-piece quality, designed down to furni-

ture and cutlery, by Arne Jacobsen, 1960–4, but additional grace notes are supplied, in the grounds, by bronzes by Henry Moore and Barbara Hepworth; the college also has one of the casts of that most inspired of Epstein's portrait heads, his *Einstein*. NUFFIELD COLLEGE has an ingenious fairly brutal open helmet-like bronze with fine fountain jets, by Hubert Dalwood; some large paintings by Ivon Hitchens, Derek Greaves and Edward Middleditch, and very beautiful glass (by John Piper and Patrick Reyntiens) in the Chapel windows, with a reredos by John Hoskin.

Of the religious establishments, MANCHESTER COLLEGE (Unitarians) has celebrated Morris glass in the Chapel, installed 1893–8 and designed by Burne-Jones. The Jesuit CAMPION HALL is much the most sumptuous in its devotional furnishings, mostly attracted to it during the charismatic reign of Father D'Arcy: they include work by Eric Gill, and large wall-paintings in rather Stanley Spencerian idiom by Charles Mahoney, with *Stations of the Cross* by Frank Brangwyn; also a remarkable Spanish late fifteenth-century monstrance, and a gilt and painted high relief of *St Ignatius Loyala with disciples*, ascribed to Juan Martinez Montañes (1568–1649).

The MAISON FRANÇAISE offers to passers-by in Norham Road a life-size bronze, *Flore*, by Maillol—a splendid Mediterranean nude, confronting even Oxford winters with warming confidence.

OPPOSITE: Sir Jacob Epstein: *Albert Einstein*. Bronze, 1932.

131

CHAPTER NINE

OTHERS

WOODSTOCK AND OXFORD

UNTIL RELATIVELY RECENTLY, THE City of Oxford got by comfortably with no local museum of consequence. Its needs might have been held—with some reason— to be met by university museums, but there were some discernible gaps. Though the Ashmolean was actively engaged in local archaeology—both on digs and in collecting and classifying finds—a museum specifically devoted to local interests, and history, was clearly a need. This was answered by the foundation (1966) of the City and County Museum (now the Oxfordshire County Museum). Its head-quarters are in Woodstock, but in 1975 it was able to open, in the former headquarters of the City Library in St. Aldate's, a much more central department, called the *Museum of Oxford*. This is virtually in sight of Carfax Tower with its clock, and attendant automatic mannikins, kilted and helmeted, that strike the quarters. The latter are in fact replacements made in 1937: the originals (unless they too are still earlier replacements of now lost originals) you can find, battered but still perky, in the Museum.

The Museum of Oxford is devised as a consecutive narra-tive of the city's history, starting from real basics (regional geological structure). It conducts the visitor deftly through to conclude him, probably mesmerised, over an enchanting display of elaborate toy-size models of fairs in full swing (all within the saloon of what was once Keble College's barge, a sturdy and handsome example of Edwardian joinery and soon doubtless to be the last surviving fabric, though no longer water-borne, of the famous picturesque College barges that once lined the river bank). The traditionalist visitor might be warned that the display uses mixed materials with gay abandon—thus the story of St. Frideswide is told in blown-up strip-cartoon idiom as if by an

American pop-artist. It is all, of course, primarily historical illustration, but studded with echoing objects: mediaeval tiles from Godstow; facsimiles of some of the more stupendous pieces of otherwise ever-invisible College plate; a wonderful sturdy wooden model of a never-used design for the Radcliffe Camera, by Hawksmoor. (If it looks a bit bashed, it has reason to do so for the children of Ditchley used it for generations as a dolls-house.) There are coins from Oxford mints, some from the Museum's collection and some lent by the Ashmolean—in fact all through there is evidence of a happy town–gown collaboration. There is a large panoramic painted view, the earliest view of Oxford, lent by the Ashmolean, and a fascinating painting of the fortifications of Oxford under siege, attributed to Jan Wyck. Perhaps the briskest and liveliest painting in view (from the City's own collection) is a late seventeenth-century account of an election in fairly obstreperous progress in the Guildhall, by Egbert van Heemskerk. Throughout, the history of the city is given fair shrift—a rare occurrence in any account of Oxford, though the University, cuckoo in the nest, is not of course neglected. This is an admirable addition to museums in Oxford.

Over the other side of St. Aldate's, and along Pembroke Street, in the highly picturesque context of an old and unspoiled town street, is an apparently unspoiled old brick warehouse which reveals itself on inspection as Oxford's *Museum of Modern Art*. This dates from 1972 in its present constitution, when the former museum of that name and the old Bear Lane Gallery amalgamated. It has no permanent exhibition, and its programme is of loan exhibitions—often three at a time, one in each of its three storeys. These can range from work of artists moving along traditional lines, like Duncan Grant or, more abstractly, William Scott, to the most way-out minimal or maximal, or way-back to photo-realism. The Museum has succeeded in establishing for itself a national, indeed international, reputation in an astonishingly short time, and its shows certainly attract national coverage in the press. It is helped by a very relaxed, unpretentious, atmosphere; by a small, comfortable coffee bar; but most of all by a highly successful adaptation of warehouse interior spaces for its new purpose. The cool expanses of the great upper room offer delightful refreshment to eye and spirit (irrespective of what's being shown there). The Museum is supported by grants from the Arts Council and the Southern Arts Association, but also, praise be, from local authorities and from some of the more enterprising colleges. Besides shows, it puts on concerts, lectures, films, poetry readings, and has a flourishing subscribing membership. It has become an essential part of the Oxford scene, and offsets the lack, in the Ashmolean permanent collections, of experimental twentieth-century art, although the new McAlpine Gallery in the Ashmolean is now committed to showing contemporary art for a third of the year.

Those who wish to visit the headquarters of the Oxford-shire County Museum must proceed some five miles northwest, to Woodstock. The Museum there is installed in Fletcher's House, in Park Street. Its special concern is with regional history and archaeology (including much industrial and agricultural archaeology), and it has an enterprising and imaginative education service that penetrates briskly throughout the area (a service which the University museums have never so far been able to offer local primary and secondary education). As far as art is concerned, the activities at Woodstock are generally confined to small shows, usually by local artists, in the Museum's Coffee Room.

In Woodstock, it is absurd not to glance at the attraction for which the town is famous throughout Britain—Blenheim, the palace of the Dukes of Marlborough.

Blenheim is a vast subject. It is also a top-runner in the country-house stakes; a whole day's outing there will give the feel of the palace, but many visits will be necessary before one begins to know it. Apart from the staterooms of the house itself, Vanbrugh's tremendous architecture enriched with sculptured adornment by Grinling Gibbons and his assistants, and the gardens and park begun by Henry Wise and opened up into marvellous contrived natural-seeming landscape by Capability Brown, can be visited again and again. The staterooms are of famous grandeur —designed perhaps in scale for some larger-than-life domesticity of Olympian beings. The hall, for instance, is sixty-seven feet high, in feeling not unlike the crossing of some secular cathedral. The ceiling is by Sir James Thornhill and carved adornments by Grinling Gibbons ("cutt Extrordingry rich and sunk very deep"). Over the door is a bust of the great 1st Duke, whose martial splendour the whole house celebrates; on a balcony over it is a whole-length painting of Queen Anne, who gave all this to the Marlboroughs, by the rare but most baroque of English-born portraitists, Edmund Lilley. There are also banners, marble, superb furniture and a bronze bust of the 9th Duke, by Epstein. In the corridors off, cases containing fine examples of rare porcelain: Meissen (gift of the King of Poland to the first Duke); Sevres; Famille Verte; Blanc de Chine.

The saloon (main dining room) has its table for ever laid for eighteen, its *trompe-l'oeil* wall painting of a columned balcony whence gossipy figures (painted by L. Laguerre) might look down on a real dinner going on below. The library is almost as grand, although it is not what it was (apart from the full-scale organ inserted by the 8th Duke in 1891). It was designed as a picture gallery, and the major paintings (other than family portraits) were sold from Blenheim at a time of financial crisis in the 1880s. Even so, this is still a noble room, and presided over by a fine statue of Queen Anne (by Rysbrack); she looks disapproving as though still somewhat put out by Sarah Duchess of Marlborough, with whom her relations degenerated to the decidedly chilly.

The sequences of staterooms are lavish and superbly splendid. The furniture, bronzes, carved looking-glasses throughout are of rich quality, but visitors will probably be most interested in the illustration of the house's successive owners in the family portraits, not least in the tapestries ordered by the 1st Duke from Brussels. These are still vividly fresh in texture and colour, and displaying in each case the Duke with his entourage poised above one of his great triumphant battles. The painted portraits do not go much earlier than the creation of the dukedom (though there are a few unusually attractive late seventeenth-century ones, and a good version of a Van Dyck double portrait). The 1st Duke himself is of course *passim*, most eloquently perhaps in Seeman's image of him discussing a battle plan with a colleague. His almost no-less-famous wife (equally embattled, if on a more domestic front) is seen most lively in a superb Kneller double portrait playing cards. Amongst the later portraits are Romneys and Reynolds and (an exotic in England) a fine haughty whole-length of the 9th Duke's Duchess Consuelo by the Parisian society painter Carolus Duran. Perhaps the most remarkable pair (Red Drawing Room) are the family groups, of the 4th Duke, by Sir Joshua Reynolds and of the 9th Duke, by John Singer Sargent.

Blenheim's chapel has a monumental memorial, by Rysbrack, to the 1st Duke. Some have accused this of stodginess, and in comparison with the full-blooded Roman baroque of Bernini (or even, in England, the swift vitality of Roubiliac) it is of course of chastened and perhaps chill movement, yet I find this pyramid of pale figures moving enough in its dignity.

ACKNOWLEDGEMENTS

The text has obviously drawn heavily on catalogues and other publications of the various museums; those in print can be obtained from the museums. I have also drawn extensively on (besides works mentioned in the text) Jennifer Sherwood and Nikolaus Pevsner, *Oxfordshire* (The Buildings of England series), 1974; Mea Allan, *The Tradescants*, 1964; Joan Evans, *Time and Chance—the Story of Arthur Evans and his Forebears*, 1943; Felix Markham, *Oxford*, 1967 (Notes by Ian Lowe). My colleagues at the Ashmolean have been unfailingly helpful, though any errors must be accounted to me and not to them. A. G. and W. O. Hassall's admirable *Treasures from the Bodleian Library*, 1976 appeared too late for me to profit from it.

LIST OF PLATES

XIV FRANS HALS (1581/5–1666), *Seated Woman.* Panel, 45 cm. × 36 cm., signed, *c.* 1660(?). Bequeathed by William Scoltock, 1886, to the Senior Common Room, Christ Church; on loan to the Picture Gallery, Christ Church.

XV THOMAS GAINSBOROUGH (1727–88) *Miss Gainsborough Gleaning, c.* 1760. Canvas, 78 cm. × 63 cm. (unfinished). Bought, with the aid of a gift in memory of Helen, Henry and Marius Winslow, 1975. Ashmolean Museum.

XVI CAMILLE PISSARRO (1830–1903) *Vue de ma Fenêtre, Eragny*, signed and dated 1888. Canvas, 65 cm. × 81 cm. Pissarro gift, 1950, to the Ashmolean Museum.

XVII J. M. W. TURNER (1775–1851) *A View of Worcester College.* Watercolours, 32 cm. × 44.3 cm., signed. For the Oxford Almanack, 1804. Lent by the Delegates of the Press to the Ashmolean Museum.

XVIII ARTHUR HUGHES (1832–1915) *Home from Sea, (A Mother's Grave).* Signed and dated 1863. Canvas, 51 cm. × 65 cm. Given by Vernon Watney, 1907, to the Ashmolean Museum.

XIX HENRI DE TOULOUSE-LAUTREC (1864–1901) *La Toilette, (Celui qui se peigne)*, signed and dated (18)91. Millboard, 58 cm. × 46 cm. Bequeathed by F. Hindley-Smith, 1939, to the Ashmolean Museum.

BLACK AND WHITE PLATES

Page 9 The Old Ashmolean (now the Museum of the History of Science). Probably designed by Thomas Wood, 1678–83. The Emperors' Heads were originally by William Bird; replaced by a new set, 1868, and again, 1972–76, by a third edition (by Michael Black).

17 JONATHAN RICHARDSON (1665–1745) *Sir Hans Sloane* in M.D. robes. Canvas, 236 cm. × 145 cm., signed and dated 1730. Given by the sitter to the University, 1731. Examination Schools.

23 E. DE CRITZ(?) *John Tradescant the Younger* in his garden, *c.* 1650. Canvas, 107 cm. × 80 cm. Given by Ashmole, 1683. Ashmolean Museum.

23 E. DE CRITZ(?), *John Tradescant the Elder.* Probably painted some time after the sitter's death (1638). Panel, 16 cm. × 14 cm. Given by Ashmole, 1683. Ashmolean Museum.

26 JOHN RILEY, *Elias Ashmole*, 1683. Canvas, 124 cm. × 101 cm. The frame is by Grinling Gibbons; the medals and decorations worn by the sitter are preserved in the Museum. Given by the sitter. Ashmolean Museum.

31 The Ashmolean Museum. South Front. By C. R. Cockerell, 1841–5.

33 EGYPTIAN, Dynasty II (*c.* 2800 B.C.): *Pharaoh Khasekhem.* Limestone (restored), 62 cm. high. From Hierakonpolis, 1908. Ashmolean Museum.

Page 34 EGYPTIAN, Late Period (*c.* 1075–333 B.C.): *Cat, sacred to the goddess Bastet.* Bronze (with gold earrings, perhaps modern). Acquired 1938. Ashmolean Museum.

35 Human skull, plastered and painted with cowrie eyes. Excavated by Dame Kathleen Kenyon in a Pre-Pottery Neolithic 'B' settlement (*c.* 7500–3000 B.C.) at Jericho, 1953. Ashmolean Museum.

35 ASSYRIAN. Eagle-headed winged figure. Marble relief, slightly larger than human scale. 9th century B.C., from the N.W. palace at Nimrod. Given by Sir Henry Layard, 1850. Ashmolean Museum.

36 CYPRUS. Bichrome IV barrel-jug, *c.* 700–600 B.C. 30.3 cm. high. Bought 1885. Ashmolean Museum.

36 Cypro-archaic *Head of a Bearded Man.* Limestone, 29.8 cm. high, 4th. century B.C. From Ruskin's collection. Given by R. G. Collingwood, 1938. Ashmolean Museum.

36 GREEK. Pelike, from Rhodes. Attic black-figure vase painting *A Shoemaker.* By the Eucharides painter. Height 40 cm. 5th century B.C. Bought 1905. Ashmolean Museum.

37 CRETE, *c.* 1400 B.C. Linear B inscription on clay-tablet (recording chariot wheels). From Knossos. Ashmolean Museum.

Page 38 CRETE, from Minoan sites. Sealstones (modern impressions, enlarged). Second millennium B.C. Ashmolean Museum.

38 GREEK. Marble idol. 77 cm. high, from a cist-grave, Amorgos (Cyclades). Early 3rd millennium B.C. Ashmolean Museum.

39 IRISH. Two lumulae, gold (perhaps used as neck ornaments). Early Bronze Age (early to middle 2nd millennium B.C.) Ashmolean Museum.

40 GREEK. Cup from Chiusi; *Boy with Hoop*, painted by the 'Colmar' painter, Attic, *c.* 500 B.C. Diam. 19.6 cm. Evans gift, 1889. Ashmolean Museum.

41 Roman copy from a lost Greek bronze statue by Polyeuktos of 280 B.C.: *Head of Demosthenes*. Marble, life scale. From Diryloeum, Turkey. Acquired 1923. Ashmolean Museum.

42 Umbrian statuette of a warrior, 5th century B.C. Bronze, 33.5 cm. tall. Given by C. D. E. Fortnum. Ashmolean Museum.

42 ROMAN. *The Emperor Lucius Verus* (A.D. 161–9). Marble bust, life-size. From Probalinthos near Marathon, late 2nd century A.D. Acquired 1947. Ashmolean Museum.

43 ROMAN. *c.* 1st century A.D. *Dancing Lar*. Bronze, inlaid with silver; 21.5 cm. high. Given by the Friends of the Ashmolean, 1970. Ashmolean Museum.

44 ROMAN. Bull, 2nd century A.D. Pipeclay terracotta, 9.5 cm. long. From Amiens, 1872. Evans gift. Ashmolean Museum.

45 ROMAN. Cupid, 2nd century A.D. Bronze, 39 cm. high. From Cirencester. From the Bodleian collection. Ashmolean Museum.

45 *The Stanton Cross, c.* A.D. 650. 4.5 cm. high. From Ixworth, Suffolk. Evans gift, 1909. Ashmolean Museum.

48 RAPHAEL (1483–1520) *Studies of two Apostles*. 49.9 cm. × 36.4 cm. Black chalk touched with white on greyish paper. Presented 1845/46. Ashmolean Museum.

Page 49 REMBRANDT VAN RIJN (1606–69), *Saskia asleep in Bed, c.* 1635. Pen and brush in bistre, 14.4 cm. × 20.8 cm. Bought, 1954, by the Ashmolean Museum.

49 MICHELANGELO (1475–1564) *Studies for the Sistine Ceiling and the Tomb of Julius II, c.* 1512/13. 286.6 cm. × 19.4 cm.; red chalk and pen with brownish ink. Presented 1845/46. Ashmolean Museum.

50 REMBRANDT VAN RIJN (1606–69), *The Artist's Studio*. 20 cm. × 19 cm., pen and ink, wash, touched with body-colour. Given by Chambers Hall, 1855, to the Ashmolean Museum.

51 FRANCESCO GUARDI (1712–93), *Venice: the Ponte di Rialto*. 22.4 cm. × 17.7 cm., pen and grey wash. Given by Chambers Hall, 1855. Ashmolean Museum.

52 GIOVANNI BATISTA PIAZZETTA (1682–1754), *Head of a Youth*. 31.5cm. × 29.9 cm., black- and -white chalks. Bought, 1934. Ashmolean Museum.

53 "MATTHIAS GRÜNEWALD". (*c.* 1475–1528), *Elderly Woman with Clasped Hands*. 37.7 cm. × 23.6 cm., charcoal. Bequeathed by Francis Douce, 1834. Ashmolean Museum.

54 ANTOINE WATTEAU (1684–1721), *A girl Seated with Music in her Lap*. 24.5 cm. × 15.8 cm., red, black, and white chalks. Given by Mrs. Emma Joseph, 1942, to the Ashmolean Museum.

55 SAMUEL PALMER (1805–81), *Self-portrait*. 29.1 cm. × 22.9 cm., black chalks heightened with white. Bought, 1932. Ashmolean Museum.

55 SAMUEL PALMER (1805–81), *The Valley with a Bright Cloud*. Pen and brush in sepia, 18.4 cm. × 27.8 cm. Signed and dated 1825. Ashmolean Museum.

60 ANDREA RICCIO (1470–1532), *Pan Listening to Echo*. Bronze, 19.3 cm. high. Bequeathed by C. D. E. Fortnum, 1899, to the Ashmolean Museum.

61 PELLEGRINO TIBALDI(?) (1527–92) or GIOVANNI DEMIO (working 1538–60), *Adoration of the Shepherds*. Panel, 120 cm. × 116 cm. Given by the National Art-Collections Fund, 1937, to the Ashmolean Museum.

INDEX

142